Kai Oidtmann

111 Places in Iceland That You Shouldn't Miss

111

emons:

English translation: John Sykes
Design: Eva Kraskes, based on a design
by Lübbeke | Naumann | Thoben
Maps: altancicek.design, www.altancicek.de
Printing and binding: CPI – Clausen & Bosse, Leck
Printed in Germany 2017
ISBN 978-3-7408-0030-7

Did you enjoy it? Do you want more?
Join us in uncovering new places around the world on:
www.111places.com

Foreword

Where would Iceland be today if the tongue-twister volcano Eyjafjallajökull had not thrust the island into the glare of global publicity in 2010 for days on end? Would Icelanders still be grappling with the financial crisis of 2008, which has now been largely overcome? This is a hypothetical question, as images of the volcano belching fire were more effective than any marketing campaign and attracted many visitors. However, during the crisis, the people of Iceland did not just rely on hordes of tourists, but got busy themselves and put ideas into practice. The salt makers of Reykjanes, for example, who produce salt using only geothermal water.

When reading this book you will keep encountering Icelanders' courage to make visions a reality, a quality that they already had before the financial crisis. This is why an 'Arctic Henge' is being built in the eastern fjords, why you can stay in a luxury hotel right next to a power station, and why the 'coolest barley' in the world grows in east Iceland. You will notice that there is no lack of strange ideas in this country when you visit the Phallus Museum, wait at a heart-shaped traffic light, enter the water library or attend a school for elves where you can learn everything about these secretive creatures. Ideas like this might be a consequence of long, dark winter days, or perhaps they are simply part of the Icelandic mentality, which was formed by the rugged landscape.

Iceland's indescribably beautiful natural environment contributes to the 111 places, of course. On the way to them you will come across a lot of fascinating stories, as beyond every bend in the road you will find superb glaciers, thundering waterfalls, interesting people or just a change in the weather.

Enjoy all of this to the full, but considerately, so that the natural world is not spoiled by us humans: tough as they sometimes appear to be, Iceland's landscapes are very vulnerable.

111 Places

1 Norðurálsvöllurinn

A stadium with a sea view

The ball boys mustn't be afraid of water here, as they have to retrieve a football from the North Atlantic in almost every game. At a distance no greater than a short pass, the waves beat on the shore behind the stand at Norðurálsvöllurinn. The football ground of ÍA Akranes is an old-style stadium. On one of its sides there is standing room on a grass bank with a fine view of the ocean. Football with the sea as a backdrop and a good playing surface are definitely to the taste of ÍA's trainer Gunnlaugur Jónsson: 'The grass recovers quickly after the winter, so by the end of April we can play outdoors again.'

Norðurálsvöllurinn, built in 1935, now holds up to 5,550 spectators. It takes its name from a sponsoring agreement with the aluminium manufacturer Norðurál from nearby Grundartangi. Previously it was simply called Akranesvöllur. On average around 1,000 fans come to the games to cheer on the Akranes players. 'In a town with a population of 6,500, that is an impressive figure,' says Haraldur Ingólfsson, the manager of ÍA, who still remembers the absolute record attendance. 'That was in 1996, when we beat KR Reykjavik 4:1 in the decisive final match of the season and won the championship. We had 6,000 supporters at that game.'

Adjoining the south side of the stadium, the Akraneshöllin was constructed a few years ago. It is a large sports hall with artificial turf that provides Gunnlaugur Jónsson's team with good training facilities all year round. 'It has taken away something of our home advantage, however, because it keeps off the wind.' Dangerous swirling crosses are therefore no longer an effective weapon for the players of ÍA Akranes – a club where the legendary Brazilian footballer Pelé has been an honorary member since 1991. In that year he presented a fair-play award to the women's team, and probably also enjoyed the sea view from Norðurálsvöllurinn.

Address Corner of Innnesvegur and Garðabraut, 300 Akranes, www.ksi.is | **Getting there**
Take route 51 towards Akranes, then on the left route 503 towards Innnes, then right along
Innnesvegur to the stadium | **Hours** Always open | **Tip** The nearby Langisandur beach is
good for a refreshing swim in the North Atlantic or a walk. It has a Blue Flag award for its
excellent water quality.

2 Akureyri Golf Club
Teeing off close to the Arctic Circle

Akureyri Golf Club, founded in 1935, is the second-oldest in Iceland, and its par 71 course is one of the most northerly 18-hole golf courses in the world. In summer, when the sun almost never sets above Akureyri, it is possible to play golf there round the clock with a magnificent mountain panorama as the backdrop. Sigmundur Ófeigsson, the club president, cannot confirm that long summer nights can be equated with long drives from the tee. Nevertheless, the bright northern nights attract many guests. 'We lend them a golf buggy and trust them to bring it back in the morning.' One of the most famous players who has done the 6,000-metre round is Jack Nicklaus, once among the world's best. 'But he was in this area mainly for the salmon fishing, not for our beautiful course,' says Sigmundur with a laugh.

Its geographical location close to the Arctic Circle comes with a few disadvantages: depending on the weather, the season only runs from late April to early October, and maintaining the fairways is a challenge. 'In summer our greenkeepers hope for lots of warm days so that they can sow new grass. In winter they battle against snow to prevent the course from being destroyed completely.' As soon as the weather allows, the 750 club members flock to the course, where a large number of trees and hills make life difficult for many of them. 'In winter they hone their technique in a hall, and in summer they play the course,' Sigmundur explains.

Altogether, some 35,000 Icelanders crowd onto the island's 67 golf courses. This makes golf the country's second most popular sport after football, and Akureyri Golf Club is not short of young talent. 'The kids take exercise outdoors, learning about patience and keeping to the rules – not only the rules of the game, but also rules of behaviour.' Which is no bad thing, both on long summer nights and on short winter days.

Address Jadar, 600 Akureyri, www.gagolf.is | Getting there From Akureyri on Ring Road 1, then on Drottningarbraut towards Hrafnagil. Just before the airport turn right onto Naustavegur, after 2 kilometres take the third exit at the roundabout into Kjarnagata, then turn right after 350 metres. | Hours End Apr–early Oct (depending on the weather) | Tip A walk over the golf course on the paths made especially for non-golfers is a good way to enjoy the natural surroundings and mountain panorama.

3 _ Heart Traffic Lights
A heart for drivers

Travellers in Iceland who arrive in Akureyri by car have often driven many miles on the Ring Road or on dusty dirt tracks without encountering a traffic light. Which is why they feel doubly welcome on reaching Akureyri when the traffic lights tell them to stop by displaying a glowing red heart.

These heart-warming traffic signals are left over from a campaign called 'Brostu með hjartanu' (Smile with your heart) that ran in 2007. In that year Iceland was particularly hard hit by the global banking crisis. Many people lost their money, their houses and their companies. 'That is why we wanted to make a statement that warms our hearts and brings back our faith in the future,' says Hulda Sif Hermannsdóttir from the town's culture and marketing office. People and companies in Akureyri could join in by hanging little hearts in their windows or printing them on their products. One year later, on the occasion of a family festival named Ein Með Öllu, many of the traffic lights in the town centre were converted to show a red heart, and they still raise the spirits of drivers who are forced to remain at a standstill for a minute. Hulda Sif no longer knows how many traffic lights shine so cordially, but she does recall a heart as large as a football pitch consisting of about 400 light bulbs. This installation beamed in winter across to Akureyri from the slopes of Vaðlaheiði, a mountain situated opposite the town. 'There are plans to revive this heart with new technology. Let's hope it will soon be shining out again.'

On Vaðlaheiði there was once a hut with a resonant name: Vaðlaheiðarvegavinnuverkfarageymsluskúr. This can be translated as 'the hut to keep tools for working on the path on the alluvial plateau'. This has no direct connection with the hearts in Akureyri, but it is regarded as one of the longest words in the Icelandic language.

Address Town centre, 600 Akureyri | Getting there On Ring Road 1 to Akureyri | Tip In Akureyri a bike and pedestrian path leads along the fjord with a fine view of the Vaðlaheiði mountain and the airport runway, a 2.4-kilometre strip of asphalt that is in the middle of the fjord and was built in 1954 at the estuary of the Eyjafjarðará.

4___Sjoppan Vöruhús
Creative items from the kiosk window

Like a child in a sweet shop who discovers something new every time – this is how visitors to the Sjoppan Vöruhús are supposed to feel. Iceland's smallest design shop, an idea of the product designer Almar Alfreðsson, is situated on Kaupvangsstræti, which locals call Arts Alley. The nickname for this steep street in the town centre is fitting. In addition to the Akureyri Art Museum, the School of Visual Arts and the studios of artists and fashion designers are based here.

In these creative surroundings, in 2014 Almar opened his design kiosk – directly beneath his workshop and apartment. From a small window in the 'shop', which has a surface area of no more than three square metres and is in fact the entrance to his house, he sells about 40 articles by designers from all over Europe. These include refurbished plastic baskets from the 1980s, cat-shaped candles with a skeleton and dolls of celebrities made by a French designer. 'I like to take new products by unknown designers. Then we can test how customers react to them,' Almar explains. After spending 12 years in Reykjavík he has returned to the north to be closer to his family. Because he lives and works under the same roof, theoretically the design kiosk is always open. 'When the door is locked, customers can ring the bell, and I open up for them.'

After completing his studies at the Science School of Art in Reykjavík, in 2011 he had the idea of making a wall sculpture with the face of Jón Sigurðsson, a man who was important in Iceland's campaign to become independent from Denmark. Almar has now produced these hand-made plaster heads in more than 30 colours and various special editions. But the owner of Iceland's smallest design shop is not yet satisfied with this. 'It is my dream that some day one of my sculptures will be hanging in every home in Iceland – or several of them.'

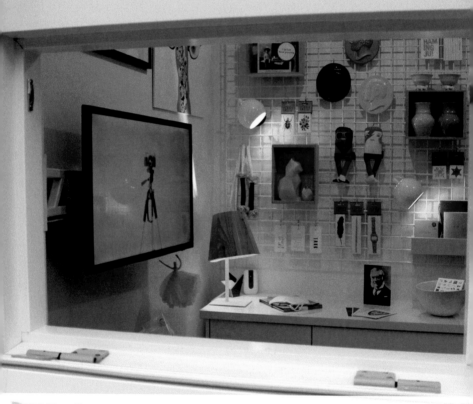

Address Kaupvangsstræti 21, 600 Akureyri | Getting there Bus 1 to Kaupvangsstræti (buses are free in Akureyri); via Ring Road 1 to Akureyri, then turn into Kaupvangsstræti. The kiosk is on the left after 220 metres. | Hours Always open | Tip At Aðalstræti 54, built in 1850, is the museum Nonni's House, the childhood home of the Icelandic author Jón 'Nonni' Sveinsson, who later wrote a dozen highly successful children's books, most of them in German. He died in Cologne in 1944.

5_ The Grocer's Shop
A trading post, then and now

The shop Steingrímsfjarðar in Norðurfjörður is a grocery, post office, petrol station, do-it-yourself store and a meeting point all at once. It is the only place to go shopping in quite a large area, and the range of goods therefore has to be extensive. Alongside joints of lamb, milk and sweets, the shelves are also filled with practical items like woolly hats, tent pegs, windscreen wipers and motor oil. This store fulfils the role that Norðurfjörður already had from the late 19th century – a trading post for the whole region. In those days the ships put in to the harbour in spring, supplying the goods that the local inhabitants had ordered the previous autumn. In return they loaded the farmers' products – usually shark-liver oil and dried fish. Back then, the trading area extended as far as Bolungarvík. Today the customers are the residents of Iceland's smallest district, Árneshreppur, tourists, and people visiting their summer houses. Unnur Guðnadóttir, a schoolgirl from Reykjavík, comes to Árneshreppur every summer to visit her grandmother and help out in the grocery store. 'It's more fun than having a holiday abroad', she says. 'I've known most people here since I was a small child, and everyone who comes shopping here usually finds time to stop for a little chat.'

In summer the goods are delivered by truck, but in winter, when the roads become impassable, they often come by air. Then it is necessary to plan ahead and send out the orders in advance so that the shelves don't become empty.

Until 1995 there were still trading ships that brought goods to Norðurfjörður. When more and more people emigrated from the region and the trading post lost its importance, these sea routes were no longer served. The grocery Kaupfélag Steingrímsfjarðar has filled the gap. Its motto is printed on the plastic bags: 'Shopping in your home region'.

Address At the petrol station in Norðurfjörður, 524 Àrneshreppur | **Getting there** Via route 61, continuing north at Hólmavík on route 643 and reaching Norðurfjörður after 94 kilometres | **Hours** Mon–Fri 9am–noon & 1–6pm, Sat & Sun 11am–3pm (in winter closed Sun) | **Tip** At the entrance to the shop is a wooden bench on which local 'celebrities' have sat and rested (see the photo on the wall by the till). It is a popular spot for customers to have a chat.

6 Hotel Djúpavík

An overnight stay in the shadow of the herring factory

The MS Suðurland lies rusting on the beach. Along with the old herring factory, it creates a forlorn scene. However, first appearances are deceptive: for more than 30 years, the red-and-white Hotel Djúpavík has been bringing life to the town. In the mid-1930s it provided accommodation for the women workers in the herring factory, and today tourists from all over the world rest here after making trips to the delightful natural environment of the Westfjords.

The surrounding mountains and the nearby waterfall are enchanting. Otherwise it would hardly be possible to explain the vision with which Ásbjörn Þorgilsson returned to his grandfather's deserted home area in 1984 to open the hotel. 'First of all we had to tidy up, clean, and then do more tidying up,' recalls his wife, Eva Sigurbjörns-dóttir. 'After the big renovation, the first guests arrived in summer 1985.' Since then Hotel Djúpavík , which now has 14 rooms, has been open continuously – at least, if the weather does not prevent guests from arriving. 'From June to October a truck delivers food and the other things that we need once a week,' says Eva, who also chairs the local council. 'For the rest of the time we have to look after ourselves.'

The two hotel owners are not the only people who enthuse about this place, which was once home to the most modern herring factory in Europe. Many guests return again and again, for example Claus Sterneck, a German visitor who first came to Djúpavík in 2003 and has organised photo exhibitions in the factory for many years. 'The buildings alone are a work of art, and ideally suited for holding exhibitions.' In summer, the cultural programme also includes concerts.

Those who leave the hotel and the herring factory after a short or long stay will have formed their own impression of the small town on its fjord, and this will undoubtedly be different from the first impression.

Address Djúpavík, 524 Árneshreppur | **Getting there** Via route 61, at Hólmavík continuing north onto route 643, then 60 kilometres to the hotel | **Hours** All year round (if the weather permits the journey) | **Tip** Climb through the small openings into the old tanks for fish oil (taking care not to get wet feet). In 2006 the Icelandic band Sigur Rós recorded the song Gitardjamm in one of them and played a concert in the herring factory.

7 Krossneslaug

A swim between the mountain and the sea

If you live next to the sea, it is a good idea to be able to swim. This applies to children above all, which is why the inhabitants of the country district of Árnes started to build an outdoor pool for swimming lessons in 1953. They did not place it next to a school, a church or some other public place, but instead selected a beach formed of rough stones to the north-east of the small settlement of Norðurfjörður. This choice of site was a sensible decision – not because of the stunning panoramic view but because the Krossneshverar, the hot springs of Krossnes, emerge from the ground above the beach. They gave the swimming pool its name, and have supplied it with water at a temperature of 64 degrees Celsius since it opened in 1954. Mixed with cold water, it flows through a pipe and enters the pool at one end, opposite the changing rooms. Swimmers who like it warm should therefore splash about in this spot or in the 'hot pot', the small Jacuzzi.

In the summer months Sigrún Sverrisdóttir lives in the small wooden hut next to the pool. She is employed as pool superintendent and lifesaver by the youth organisation Leifur Heppni, the operator of Krossneslaug. 'In the last 60 years hardly anything has changed, apart from the number of visitors,' she says. 'In 2014 about 6,000 people came to bathe here in the summer months.'

Outside the tourist season she looks in just once a week to clean the changing rooms and toilets. 'Yet it is much nicer here in winter than in summer. It is simply wonderful to float in the hot water on your own while watching the northern lights in the sky.

In this season the swimming pool is used mainly by local people. 'There are not many of them – only about 40 people live here. We are the smallest district in Iceland.' She laughs, and can hardly wait for the next winter to arrive.

Address At the end of road 6401, 524 Árneshreppur | **Getting there** Via route 61, continuing north at Hólmavík onto the 643. After 93 kilometres turn left onto the 6401 and drive to the end, following the signs to the pool: Krossneslaug. | **Hours** Always open | **Tip** On the way from Krossneslaug to Djúpavík, on route 61 you pass a private museum of art and crafts called Kört. It is in a small place called Árnes and has been run by Valgeir Benediktsson since 1997. His works made from driftwood and old items found in the area are on display.

8__ The Museum of Melodies
Keeping the memory of Icelandic hits

Jón Kristján Ólafsson floats across the carpets of his house in
Bíldudalur in a gracious manner. You can tell by watching him that
he was once used to standing on stage in front of a large audience
and knows how to take possession of a space. His slippers and the
Elvis patches on his red pullover do nothing to lessen the charisma
of this ageing pop singer. He has turned the basement rooms into
a Museum of Melodies. The walls, tables and chests of drawers, the
bathroom and even the kitchen, in other words practically all the
available surfaces, are decorated with LPs, autograph cards, old stage
costumes and photos of times gone by. On the records and pictures
inside glass frames, the visitor keeps coming across the faces of
Iceland's hit singer Ragnar Bjarnason and singer-songwriter Haukur
Morthens. Jón Kristján especially seems to treasure the memory of
Elly Vilhjálms. He sits contentedly on the sofa and listens to her
gentle voice, which comes from the speakers of a record player that
is turned up to disco volume.

Jón Kristján once worked with a great number of stars of the past.
His band was called Facon, and they played for several years in the
1960s. They performed in the famous Art Deco-style Hotel Borg in
Reykjavík, then a fashionable place to go dancing. Marlene Dietrich
drank a cocktail or two here in the 1940s.

Jón Kristján no longer goes on stage for big audiences, but he still
performs – as in 2011, when he invited Ragnar Bjarnason, the grand
old man of Icelandic pop songs, for a concert in his garden, and
hundreds of people came to listen. On most days, things are quiet in
the Museum of Melodies. It is worth paying him a visit, even though,
or because, Jón Kristján does not speak a great deal of English. He
shows his visitors around using expressive gestures, as befits a man
with a past in show business.

Address Tjarnarbraut 5, 465 Bíldudalur, +354 847-2542 | **Getting there** Route 63 to
Bíldudalur, turn off onto Dalbraut and pass the town boundary. The museum is on the
left a little way beyond the petrol station. | **Hours** June–Sept Mon–Fri 1–6pm, Sat & Sun
by arrangement | **Tip** The Icelandic Sea Monster Museum is a few paces away on the other
side of the road. It tells lots of scary stories. Children can hunt sea beasts on an interactive
'monster table'.

9_ Samúel's Sculptures
Naïve art on Eagle Fjord

A Byzantine church tower and a replica of the Lion Fountain in the Alhambra exude a touch of Mediterranean atmosphere. They stand in the remote Selárdalur valley and belong to the house of Samúel Jónsson, who died in 1969. At the end of the Arnarfjörður, the farmer Jónsson set up house after retiring and began a second career as a sculptor – not an easy task for a man in his declining years, as he had to carry most of the materials for his sculptures up from the beach with his own hands. He used sand, water and cement to create seals, lions and people, and he even constructed a church. This was not so much a matter of his faith as of his defiant attitude: when he donated a painting to the church in Selárdalur for its 100th anniversary, the congregation declined to accept the gift. Samúel's response was simply to build his own church to house the picture.

When the German sculptor Gerhard König came to the Selárdalur valley as a tourist in 1997, he found the artist's legacy in a state of decay. A year later he became a member of Félag um listasafn Samúels Jónssonar í Selárdal, the association of friends of the sculptor's work, and a year later restored the first statue of a lion with the help of old photos.

'When you look at Samúel's sculptures, you may be able to tell that he never trained as an artist. Nevertheless, I have great respect for his work, which he carried out passionately until his 85th year.'

Samúel had little ploys to overcome the process of ageing. A shell path led down to the beach from his house. The brightness of the shells helped his fading eyes to find the way.

Since 2004, Gerhard König has made his way to the Westfjords for a few weeks every summer. He organises a work camp to preserve the quirky houses, the simple statues and the church. 'Samúel was an artist with the heart of a child, and he deserves it.'

Address Brautarholt in Selárdalur, 465 Bíldudalur | **Getting there** Via route 63 towards Bíldudalur, crossing the town on Dalbraut and continuing on route 619 for 23 kilometres to Selárdalur | **Tip** On the way from Bíldudalur to Selárdalur, you pass several pagan graves on the right, which probably date back to the 10th century. Excavations since 2006 have uncovered human bones, grave goods and the remains of a ship.

10___The Seven Waterfalls
Quiet or thundering

In the Westfjords the water of the river Dynjandisá has created a dramatic natural feature. At this place seven waterfalls, Dynjandi, Hæstahjallafoss, Strompgljúfrafoss, Göngumannafoss, Hrísvaðsfoss, Hundafoss and Bæjarfoss, plunge into the valley below. Nowhere else in Iceland can this natural spectacle be seen seven times in one place.

The most impressive of the seven is Dynjandi, whose foaming white water falls like a veil over the shoulders of a bride. The terraces of Dynjandi, which is about 100 metres high, are the result of an ice age approximately 10,000 years ago. In that era, huge glaciers cut deep fjords into the land and the force of their ice carved small promontories out of the basalt and lava stone, which have differing degrees of hardness. The various layers can still be identified at the side of the waterfall. At its top edge Dynjandi is some 30 metres wide, at its base a good 60 metres. Since 1981 it has been a protected natural feature, and its name means 'the thunderer'.

The quiet sounds along the other waterfalls are no less remarkable than the impressive noise of Dynjandi. After every bend in the path, the rushing sound changes, sometimes vanishing altogether but then becoming stronger again as you approach the next of the seven waterfalls. When you then reach Dynjandi, the crashing wall of water is a captivating spectacle. Here it is worth taking a look back. The peaceful valley and the Arnarfjörður make a lovely contrast to the constant change and roar of Dynjandi. The masses of water, which we admire today as a fascinating natural spectacle, were a source of difficulties for farmers in past times. Landslides and floods repeatedly destroyed valuable grazing land. This is why they tried to protect their land with barriers of stone – in case 'the thunderer' became too thunderous once again.

Address Vestfjarðavegur in Arnarfjörður, about 60 kilometres north-east of 465 Bíldudalur |
Getting there From Flókalundur via route 60 towards Þingeyri. You reach Dynjandi after
31 kilometres. | **Tip** The famous Icelander Jón Sigurðsson was born in Hrafnseyri on
17 June, 1811. He is regarded as the pioneer of Iceland's independence from Denmark.
A small museum was built in his honour. You find it by taking route 60 towards Þingeyri,
21.5 kilometres further on from Dynjandi.

11 Bolafjall
Iceland's ear

Thanks to its exposed location at the north-western tip of Iceland, the region around Bolungarvík became an attractive site as a military listening post in the 20th century. Today, the gleaming grey sphere of the radar station on the plateau of Bolafjall Mountain still testifies to this. It was constructed in 1992 in connection with Iceland's membership of NATO and is now operated by the Icelandic coastguard. It has a significant role in monitoring and controlling air traffic in a radius of up to 460 kilometres. Important communication units, which are used by a number of different NATO partners, are housed in the station.

In World War II this region was already used as a listening post. On the other side of the fjord, the British army built a base on the mountain called Grænahlíð in order to watch over the straits that separate Iceland from Greenland. Very close by, on the summit of neighbouring Straumnesfjall, the US army stationed troops during the Cold War to monitor Soviet activities in the air and on the water. In 1958 a radar station went into operation on the base, but had to be closed only two years later for financial reasons.

In contrast to the capabilities of the radar station, visitors to Bolafjall have to rely on their naked eyes or perhaps on a pair of binoculars. But whether they arrive with or without technical assistance, the coast of Greenland is not visible from the top of Bolafjall, however clear the weather is. The rumour that you can see it continues to circulate stubbornly, but owing to the curvature of the earth, a view of Greenland is neither practically nor theoretically possible. Mirror effects of the atmosphere, which are frequent in polar regions, may be the reason for this myth. Nevertheless, at a height of 630 meters, Bolafjall in the Westfjords indisputably provides a wonderful view.

LOKAÐ

Address On route 630, 415 Bolungarvík | Getting there Via route 61 to Bolungarvík, then
turn left into Skólastígur, which continues as Skálavíkurvegur, and after 5.5 kilometres drive
to Bolafjall on the right | Hours Open during summer months (in bad weather the road
may be closed) | Tip On the slopes of the mountain Traðarhyrna, north of Bolungarvík,
stand two anti-avalanche walls, totalling almost 1,000 metres in length. These impressive
structures are called Vörður and Vaki – guardian and watchman.

12 ‒ The Stórurð
Walking for honours

A number of pearls lie hidden in the Fljótsdalshérað region in the east of Iceland. They may not be the kind of pearls that make a woman's heart melt, but they are a delight to nature lovers: waymarked walking routes to the most interesting places in the region.

One of these is the Stórurð, a site of large rocks scattered across the fascinating landscape west of Dyrfjöll, a mountain in eastern Iceland. Between them, milky-green ponds of water shine. On the way there, you walk past green meadows and snow-covered summits. A total of 26 sights, which can be reached on the signposted walking routes, are listed by the association Ferðafélags Fljótsdalshéraðs. They include the Hengifoss waterfall and Snæfell, a mountain with a height of 1,833 metres. In 2007 a member of the club, Hjördís Hilmarsdóttir, placed a small wooden box with a rubber stamp, a visitors' book and information about the place at each of these sights. In the tourist office at Egilsstaðir or from the association you can buy maps and put a stamp on them when you have hiked to one of the 26 sights. 'The aim of this was to attract more families to the beautiful natural surroundings of Egilsstaðir', Hjördís explains.

Originally, 18 walking routes led to the pearls of Fljótsdalshérað. The interest of walkers was so great that a further eight tours were added to the list. Some of them are easy routes that take only two or three hours. For others you need to plan half a day or a whole day, and they may include significant ascents and descents.

All those who collect nine stamps or more in the course of a walking season can hand in their map to the walkers' association and take part in a competition in September. Furthermore, all walkers who successfully reach the sites can have their names included in a kind of list of honour, and are then entitled to call themselves 'Fljótsdalshérað sprinters'.

Address Route 94 (walkers' car park), 720 Borgarfjörður eystri | Getting there Via route 94. The starting point is 17 kilometres west of Borgarfjörður eystri. | Tip The association Ferðafélags Fljótsdalshéraðs has produced a list of 22 remote farms on the Jökuldalsheiði plateau to make this upland region more attractive for visitors. This information is available in the tourist centre.

13__ The Automobile Club

A presidential limousine at a preferential price

The first car that the German chancellor Angela Merkel owned in the West, a white 1990 model VW Golf II, changed hands a few years ago for more than 10,000 euros. Yet the fact that prominent previous owners do not necessarily make the value of car go through the roof is now known to members of the Fornbílafjelag Borgarfjarðar automobile club. In early 2013 they acquired an attractive bargain when they bought a car that had belonged to Vigdís Finnbogadóttir, formerly president of Iceland, for the token price of one króna (about 0.01 euro). It was not until the purchase of the Toyota Crown Royal Saloon with a little crown on the radiator had been completed that they realised who had owned it, says Gunnar Jónsson, a member of the club. 'In the official papers there were three other owners and the name of a car dealer, and so we did not notice Vigdís' name until later.'

The car is now in the club premises on Bráqarey, a small island off Borgarnes, and can be visited, just like the members' other classic cars. 'We only cleaned it, and otherwise left the car in the condition in which we bought it,' says Gunnar. The silver limousine has an almost complete set of fittings, and was even equipped with a cassette recorder capable of making recordings when Vigdís Finnbogadóttir owned it. She was the world's first democratically elected female head of state, and must have had good ideas that needed to be recorded when she was at the wheel.

In 1988 the Toyota Crown Royal Saloon was a top-of-the-mid-range car that probably cost around 25,000 euros. It has found a new home in a hall belonging to Fornbílafjelag Borgarfjarðar, where it enjoys good company.

Visitors can see a Ford Model T (also known as the Tin Lizzie) made in 1927, a pink East German Trabant and a total of 30 other cars – ranging from big American limousines to small British cars.

Address Vigdís Crown Royal Saloon, Brákarbraut on Brákarey, 310 Borgarnes | **Getting there** Via Ring Road 1, turn onto Borgarbraut and its continuation Brákarbraut, cross the bridge to Brákarey after 1.3 kilometres, then turn left after 200 metres | **Hours** June–Aug Mon–Sun 1–5pm, Sept–May Sat 1–5pm | **Tip** On a hill next to the bridge to Brákarey, a sculpture commemorates the woman after whom the island is named: Þorgerður Brák. In Egil's Saga she saves Egil from his choleric father Skalla-Grímur, whom she drives into the sea.

14 Bjössaróló
A playground made from old boards

What would the authorities in most western countries say if a retired craftsman were to build a children's playground using second-hand boards? Björn Hjörtur Guðmundsson presumably gave little thought to questions like that in 1979, when he began to construct Bjössaróló. Nevertheless, it goes without saying that the well-being and safety of the children were important to him. To this day visitors can gain an impression of the inventiveness and skill of this master carpenter from Borgarnes.

The playground is situated on a hill-covered promontory, right by the sea. Through the years Björn, who was referred to as Bjössi, filled the site with colourful swings, see-saws and climbing frames. Bushes, trees and little paths give the children plenty of opportunities to work off their energy, and the playground equipment, though now old, still fulfils its purpose.

The natural environment was important to Bjössi, who has now passed away, and he therefore tried to communicate his philosophy to those who go to the playground – in a playful manner. He painted proverbs on signs and placed them in different places in Bjössaróló so that the children could learn them by heart. In this way he reminded them that it is better to let flowers grow than to pick them.

In 1992 Vigdís Finnbogadóttir, the Icelandic president, honoured Bjössi's committed work and tried out one of his swings in person. A photo of this visit can be seen on a plaque on the playground. After Bjössi's death in 1998 the weather caused the playground equipment to deteriorate. Without the loving care of the old carpenter, it began to decay. Not until 2008 was Bjössaróló restored to its former condition with donations amounting to 2.5 million króna (about 17,500 euros). Since then it has once again been possible for the children to enjoy the swings, slides and see-saws the way Bjössi liked it.

Address Near Skúlagata, at the corner of Helgugata, 310 Borgarnes | Getting there Via Ring Road 1, turn onto Borgarbraut and its continuation Brákarbraut, park on the right after 11 kilometres, follow the coast path and the signs to Bjössaróló | Hours Always open | Tip Only 500 metres away is Skallagrímsgarður, a small park that plays a part in Egil's Saga. According to the story, the father of Egil Skallagrímsson, hero of the saga, is buried there.

15 Hallormsstaður Forest

'Norwegian Wood'? No, an Icelandic forest

On the drive from Egilsstaðir, as you head south along the bank of Lake Lagarfljót, sooner or later you will notice a gradual change in the natural surroundings. This starts with occasional shrubs, followed by small groups of trees, and before long you are in the middle of one of Iceland's largest forest areas. Hallormsstaður Forest covers about 740 hectares and serves as a place of recreation for both locals and tourists. 'We have walking trails here with a total length of 40 kilometres,' says Þröstur Eysteinsson from the forestry office.

'The forest also surrounds the village of Hallormsstaður, the only one in Iceland that is in the middle of woodland.' In 1905 the remains of a small birch wood were given protected status here, making Hallormsstaður Forest the first of what are now 53 state forests. This was also the start of the campaign for the forestation of Iceland. Between 1990 and 2009 this reached a climax, with the planting of four to six million saplings per year. The trees that grow in Hallormsstaður today are mainly birch, larch and different species of fir and pine. 'But the tallest tree here is a black poplar,' says Þröstur. 'In 2014 it was 25 metres high.' By Icelandic standards this is an impressive size.

In 1984 a big name from the world of music paid a visit to Hallormsstaður. The Beatles' drummer Ringo Starr looked in at a music festival in Atlavík. Þröstur relates that an amusing encounter then took place, in which alcohol consumption might possibly have played some part.

'When Ringo went to the stage with the Icelandic band Stuðmenn, a man from the crowd came up to shake his hand, and asked: "Hey, Peter, my old teacher from Eiðar, do you still recognise me?"' How Ringo reacted to this is not recorded, but since then it has been known in Iceland that there was once a teacher who looked like Ringo Starr.

Address Hallormsstaður Forest, 701 Egilsstaðir | **Getting there** Ring Road 1 to Lagarfljótsee, then route 931 towards Hallormsstaður. The wood is about 20 kilometres south-west of Egilsstaðir. | **Tip** Between the Hallormsstaður Hotel and the idyllic Atlavík campsite lies an arboretum, a collection of different trees. Signs give information about the 85 species.

16_Húsey Riding Centre
Living in harmony with nature

'Ah, that's what milk tastes like!' Örn Þorleifsson frequently experiences this reaction and surprised faces when his guests try milk fresh from the cow. In addition to the cow, he has 30 sheep, horses and a few hens; he tries to live from what nature provides. 'We also have a pigeon in case the post fails to arrive,' he jokes. And, depending on the weather, that is not an unlikely event. Húsey is a horse-riding centre, approximately 60 kilometres from Egilsstaðir between two glacial rivers. It is paradise for nature lovers. Visitors can discover many kinds of birds and plants, and also observe seals on the sand banks nearby. In spring and autumn, even reindeer come to the plains around Húsey.

In 1970 Örn leased the farm. Eleven years later he opened a guesthouse and started to run horse treks. 'We see seals on almost every excursion. This delights the tourists who come to us from the cruise ships in Seyðisfjörður.' These are the only times when life at Húsey is bustling. Otherwise it is a place of profound tranquillity. The guests seem to like this. 'Some of them have been here more than 20 times and have now become more like friends.'

The grey-haired farmer Örn also maintains a friendly relationship to his animals. He breeds some of his horses himself, and also breaks them in for riding. 'If a horse doesn't want to carry a rider whatever we do, then we don't try to force it.' His reaction is considerably more vigorous when the subject of the Kárahnjúkar power station is mentioned. In order to provide electricity for an aluminium plant in Reyðarfjörður, the two glacial rivers that surround Húsey were dammed in the highlands. This is a threat to the habitats of many animals. The seals are especially affected. 'The dam is the craziest structure in the whole of Europe,' Örn complains – a note of sourness that contrasts with his sweet milk.

Address At the end of route 926, 701 Egilsstaðir | Getting there Ring Road 1, turn onto route 925, after 9 kilometres continue straight ahead on route 926 and follow the road to the end. Húsey is about 55 kilometres north of Egilsstaðir | Hours Early Jan to early Dec | Tip On the way to Húsey, the reconstructed turf church Geirsstaðakirkja lies at Hróarstunguvegur. In 1997 the remains were discovered in excavations. The original probably dates from the Viking era (c. 930–1260).

17 __ The Lagarfljót Monster
Truth, myth or a figment of the imagination?

The shape of Lake Lagarfljót in eastern Iceland has a slight resemblance to a long worm. This may be the reason why the notorious Lagarfljót monster seems to have felt quite at home in its waters for several centuries. Since 1345 there have been repeated reports of sightings of the beast. Descriptions of its appearance vary greatly. Its length is said to be between a few metres and several kilometres. When a telephone cable was laid through the lake in 1983, sounds made by the monster were supposedly recorded in the depths.

A real myth has now developed around the creature in the lake. A 13-person 'truth commission' contributed to this in 2014 when it declared that video recordings made by the farmer Hjörtur Kjerúlf were genuine. Two years earlier he had succeeded in filming the alleged Lagarfljót monster. His extremely shaky video shows a snake-like movement beneath the surface of the water – and nothing more. The footage nevertheless attracted millions of clicks on the internet, and television teams from the United States, Japan and Canada arrived in Iceland, trying in vain to track the monster down in its home waters.

As far as the authenticity of Hjörtur's video is concerned, opinions differ. The theories about what can be seen on his film range from old fishing nets and knotted plastic bags to a remote-controlled underwater device. Despite all doubts that have been expressed, the myth of the Lagarfljót monster refuses to die. It is worth making your own trip there to look for it. Countless little bays in beautiful natural surroundings afford a good view across the water, and signs all around the lake mark the places where the monster is said to have appeared. And there is no need to be fearful, as the creature in Lake Lagarfljót does not seem to be at all dangerous. No reports have ever been received that it eats humans.

Address Lagarfljót, 701 Egilsstaðir | Getting there Ring Road 1 to Egilsstaðir | Tip South of Lake Lagarfljót stands Skriðuklaustur, once the home of the Icelandic poet Gunnar Gunnarsson. The manor house has striking white-pointed masonry and a grass roof. Today it houses an arts centre and a café.

18 Móðir Jörð Farm
Mother Earth's treats

Eymundur Magnússon had firmly made up his mind by the age of seven: he wanted to be a farmer. Although he was born in Reykjavík, he was attracted to the countryside, and in 1979 he started to breed cattle on a farm near Egilsstaðir. As he always preferred brown fields to green meadows, in 1985 he switched to an organic farm called Móðir Jörð (Mother Earth). Over the years he planted about one million trees on his 400 hectares of land in order to give the soil and plants better protection from the weather.

'In this way we have created our own microclimate, and the ground is warmer.' In addition to 25 to 30 different kinds of salad plants, vegetables and herbs, Eymundur cultivates barley. 'The coolest barley in the world,' he laughs, as fields of barley are an exotic sight in Iceland. This grain was planted in Iceland as long ago as the 9th century, but at some stage its cultivation was forgotten. Thanks to a kind of seed corn that is used in Scandinavia, he succeeded in raising his yield and putting barley back on the menu of the Icelandic people.

Some 80 interns from all over the world help all year round on the farm's fields, where everything takes longer to ripen than in other countries. But this slow growth is by no means detrimental to the quality, says Sveinn Kjartansson, a television chef who is among the celebrity customers of Móðir Jörð. 'The colours of the products are not always very intense, but the taste definitely is.'

Eymundur's wife, Eygló Björk Ólafsdóttir, also shows good taste when she makes fruit into jam and vegetables into chutney, or bakes bread from the grain grown on the farm. These lovingly made treats are sold on the farm, of course. And because delicious products deserve an attractive presentation, Eymundur is planning to build a little shop – entirely from the wood of Icelandic trees that he planted himself 30 years ago.

Address Vallanes, 701 Egilsstaðir | Getting there Via Ring Road 1 to Lagarfljótsee, then route 931 towards Hallormsstaður, turning right after 1.5 kilometres right and following the track to the farm (about 15 kilometres south-west of Egilsstaðir) | Hours May–Sept Mon–Sat 9am–6pm | Tip The 'monster path' branches off from the path to Móðir Jörð farm. This short trail leads through romantic woods and contains a few surprises, including a red wooden bed. Of course, monsters many be lurking everywhere.

19__Street Signs
Where the streets have French names

In Fáskrúðsfjörður the harbour road is not merely called Hafnargata, but also bears the name 'Rue du Port'. This is not an isolated case: a French translation has been added to many street names in this small town. The reason is not that the officials in the local government have been drinking too much Bordeaux, but that close links to France are deeply rooted in the history of the town.

In the mid-19th century, French seamen went out in search of new fishing grounds to satisfy the huge demand for seafood in France. Some of them came from Dunkirk and Gravelines, in France's Nord département, and Paimpol in Brittany, and they found what they were looking for off Iceland. This caused suffering to many fishermen's families, as the voyage was dangerous. It is estimated that between the early 19th century and the early 20th century, more than 4,000 French seamen lost their lives off Iceland.

Of course, the presence of many Frenchmen had an effect on ports like Fáskrúðsfjörður, where the fishing boats landed their catch. The locals knitted hats, gloves and pullovers for the crews in exchange for other goods. The conditions of work on the boats were tough. As a result, many fishermen fell ill or sustained injuries, and the French navy sent special hospital ships. With the permission of the Danish government, which governed Iceland at that time, the French even built a hospital in Fáskrúðsfjörður at the end of the 19th century. A Catholic chapel, a house for the doctor, a mortuary and a cemetery, in which the graves of 49 French seamen can be seen, followed.

Other buildings dating from those years were restored or returned to their original location between 2010 and 2014 as part of the 'French Project'. Today they are used to house a hotel, offices and a store. Only the small chapel now serves its original purpose. It is still in use as a church.

Address Hafnargata, 750 Fáskrúðsfjörður | Getting there Via routes 92 and 96 | Tip In the former house of the doctor (Hafnargata 12) there is an exhibition about the historic links between France and Fáskrúðsfjörður. It includes an underground tunnel that looks like the inside of an old fishing boat and conveys a good impression of the hard life of the sailors (May–Aug daily 10am–6pm or by arrangement, +354 470-9000).

20_ The Nonsense Museum
From police headgear to sugar lumps

'What's nonsense and what isn't usually depends on your point of view,' Valdemar Jónsson explains. He should know, because he runs the Dellusafnið, the Nonsense Museum, in Flateyri. 'Things that have no value at all for one person are collected with great passion by someone else.' And when you take a tour of his exhibition, this becomes clear: cigarette packs, matchboxes, teaspoons, police caps, model cars, crown corks, labels from wine bottles and sugar lumps, most of it meticulously lined up on shelves and in glass cases.

The Nonsense Museum was founded in 2010 by Jón Svanberg Hjartarson, a former policeman. He added more than 100 policeman's caps and a lot of police badges from all over the world to the collection. The current director of the museum, Valdemar, was gripped by collecting fever in 1997. 'I bought an excavator for my construction company, and it came with a miniature model as a gift.' His collection is now so large that he presents it in the museum in the form of model landscapes – with sand, stones and everything else that you see on a building site. He is particularly proud of three small-scale trucks that he has painted in the same colours as his real vehicles.

A glance at the showcase filled with miniature liqueur and spirits bottles makes it clear that a passion for collecting involves a lot of discipline. Valdemar's wife Nilma has gathered them on their travels. 'This is one of the most endangered collections of all,' Valdemar quips. 'But thank heavens, my wife never drinks alcohol.' Collecting seems to be in the family genes: his daughter Hrefna has contributed an array of ball-point pens.

Whether this is nonsense or not, most visitors leave the museum with a smile on their faces, says Valdemar. 'It's only small children who are not always pleased, because they can't touch the construction vehicles behind glass and play with them.'

Address Hafnarstræti 11, 425 Flateyri, +354 893-3067 | Getting there Via route 60 towards Flateyri. Turn onto route 64 there. In the town centre, Hafnarstræti goes off to the left. | Hours 1 June to 20 Aug, daily 1–5pm or by appointment | Tip At the entrance to Flateyri is the Tankurinn, an old tank for fish oil, now converted to a summer house but once a sound studio in which Icelandic bands such as GusGus recorded their albums.

21_The Aluminium Smelter
Energy guzzlers under fire

Like two huge pieces of candy from dreamland, two red-and-white-striped aluminium oxide silos stand on Reykjanesbraut near Hafnarfjörður. In 1969, Iceland's first aluminium smelting plant opened for production there. At that time it was owned by a Swiss company, Alusuisse, and now its owner is the Canadian multinational Rio Tinto Alcan. About 450 employees produce 185,000 tonnes of aluminium per year. The long production sheds are nothing extraordinary – in many parts of Europe the inhabitants are used to much larger industrial installations. Nevertheless, Icelanders have mixed feelings about the aluminium plants in their country and the factories' foreign owners.

'The smelters require enormous quantities of energy, which are provided by the state at low prices', criticises the blogger Helga Katrín Tryggvadóttir. 'Apart from that, the raw material, aluminium oxide, has to be imported by ship from the USA or Ireland.' She and environmental organisations like Saving Iceland have been campaigning for some time now against the construction of more and more aluminium plants. Although the energy is gained from hydroelectric or geothermal sources, the bore holes and dams of the additional power stations damage the natural environment. Opponents of the industry also make the criticism that the companies pay too little tax in Iceland and pass on the profits to their parent companies abroad by manipulating the balance sheet.

For the sake of a few thousand jobs, in the past some politicians have sold Iceland's environment cheaply – with expensive consequences.

Despite this, plans for new aluminium smelters are presented again and again. Whether they are implemented depends on politicians, the inhabitants' opposition and perhaps on Saving Iceland or Helga Katrín. Otherwise Iceland will continue to be a dream location for aluminium producers.

Address Reykjanesbraut, 221 Hafnarfjörður | Getting there Via route 41 | Hours Can only be viewed from the outside | Tip Inland from the aluminium smelter lies the perfectly straight track of the Kvartmílu Klúbburinn motor sports club. In summer, races are held on the 'quarter mile', which is a two-lane metalled track.

22 Hellisgerði Park
Where elves, birds and cats meet

At first glance Hafnarfjörður looks little different from other small towns in Iceland. But if you look more closely, between the buildings and the streets you will discover many small lava rocks – home to elves, trolls and other mystical creatures. Hafnarfjörður is famous for its large population of elves – partly because of Hellisgerði Park. Here the lava field on which the town was built breaks through to the surface, covered in trees, grass and moss. Narrow paths lead across this small area between hills.

In 1922 a local association called Magni had the idea of creating a park for recreation that would also be home to rare plants from the surroundings of Hafnarfjörður. It was not long before agreement was reached with the town authorities for the use of a piece of land by the Fjarðarhellir – the fjord cave, which can still be seen in the park. The name Hellisgerði – cave garden – is derived from this.

Many hidden beings are said to have made their homes in the twisted lava formations, which means that the chances of meeting elves and trolls are particularly high here. On a guided tour of the site, visitors are informed about the best spots for such an encounter and can learn all about the *huldufólk* and their place in the culture of Iceland.

Those who are not interested in creatures from other worlds can enjoy the flora and fauna. More than a dozen kinds of trees, some of them extremely rare in Iceland, grow in the park. The copper beeches, common Douglas fir and grey poplars are home to many birds – including the gold crest. With a body length of about nine centimetres it is one of the smallest birds in Europe. The trees attract the birds, and the birds in turn attract cats. If you stroll there in good weather it will not be long before a cat turns up – to hunt for birds and elves, or perhaps to accompany visitors on their walk.

Address Reykjavíkurvegur, at the corner of Skúlaskeið, 220 Hafnarfjörður | Getting there Bus 1 to Hellisgerði or Sjónarhóll; via route 40 or 41, in Hafnarfjörður turn onto Flatahraun towards the town centre, then left onto Reykjavíkurvegur. There is a small car park at the corner of Skúlaskeið right next to Hellisgerði | Hours Always open | Tip The walk to Víðistaðatún Park takes 10 minutes. After an arts festival in 1991, artists from various countries donated the 16 sculptures that are on display.

23__ Straumsvík Bay
The beauty of lava and cold springs

On the bay of Straumsvík, to the west of Hafnarfjörður, beauty and ugliness lie close together: on the one hand the aluminium smelter run by Rio Tinto Alcan, on the other a wonderful natural feature, the lava field of Hrútagjárdyngja. It originated 6,000 to 7,000 years ago and shaped the coast between the bays of Straumsvík and Vatnsleysuvík. Its total volume is estimated at approximately three cubic kilometres. To the west of the aluminium plant a bumpy track leads into the lava field and the old farmhouse of Straumur, built in 1927 by the state architect Guðjón Samúelsson. In 1986 the municipality of Hafnarfjörður bought the building, which now houses the studios of a number of artists.

The coastline at Straumsvík is very rugged. At low tide, little lagoons and pools form. Then you can see the cold-water springs from which large quantities of fresh water flow into the sea. The water comes from precipitation in the interior that trickles through the porous stone of the lava field and flows towards the sea along natural channels. In 2010 the Iceland GeoSurvey Institute estimated the water flow at about 4,000 litres per second.

A number of different species of small birds nest and hatch their eggs here on the land, in addition to gulls, eider ducks, geese and ptarmigans. A few years ago the area around Straumsvík was known as a breeding ground for terns, but today these birds are seen much more rarely. The reason for this could be the increasing number of American mink, which have a great liking for terns in their diet.

You can also discover the remains of farm buildings scattered across the lava field. Some of them have fallen into decay, while others seem to be in use as summer houses. The oldest archaeological finds date from the 12th or 13th century, when the surroundings of Straumsvík presented a picture of nothing but beauty without any ugliness.

Address Óttarstaðavegur, 221 Hafnarfjörður | Getting there Ring Road 1 to Reykjavík, then take route 41 towards Hafnarfjörður and turn right after 15.5 kilometres immediately beyond the aluminium plant onto a dirt track (not the approach to the factory) | Tip The association Umhverfissjóður Verslunarinnar has marked several fine walking trails of different lengths through the lava field with wooden posts. One starting point is only 60 metres from the old Straumur farmhouse.

24__Jökulsárlón
Where the glacier calves

Was the musician Peter Licht thinking of Iceland's glacier lagoon named Jökulsárlón when he wrote the lyrics of his song Sonnendeck? 'Where the glacier calves, where the seconds fly into the blue sea,' he sings, and that is what happens to seconds on the shore of Jökulsárlón. Time flies there, and you can hardly get enough of the sight of icebergs on the lagoon. Different shapes, sizes and colours appear in ceaseless succession when light is refracted by the crystals – from snow white to ice blue and lava grey. The different shades of colour come from the varying proportion of air contained in these fragments, which are thousands of years old. Ice with a low air content shimmers blue; if the crystals have enclosed many little bubbles of air, they reflect white light; traces of lava lend a dark hue.

At the edge of the lagoon, which is up to 150 metres deep, you feel as if you are standing in front of an open refrigerator. The coldness of the icebergs radiates as they slowly drift down what must be Iceland's shortest river and break apart with an ominous cracking noise. Crashing sounds can often be heard in the distance, when another piece of Norðlingalægðarjökull, the eastern part of Breiðamerkurjökull, splashes into the lagoon. This natural spectacle is a constant reminder of climate change, as Jökulsárlón arose only through the warming of the earth's atmosphere in the 20th century.

The glacier lagoon, on which tours with amphibious vehicles and rubber boats operate, is undoubtedly one of Iceland's greatest attractions. No visitor should miss this fascinating scene, as climate change means that Jökulsárlón will continue to change and one day will no longer have its present appearance. Or, in the words of Peter Licht: 'Everything that exists lasts three seconds. One second beforehand, one second afterwards, one for the middle of it all.'

Address Þjóðvegur in southern Iceland, about 80 kilometres south-west of 781 Höfn | Getting there Go south on Ring Road 1 | Tip It is worth walking to the nearby beach, where the waves drive blocks of ice ashore, and the brightness of the ice makes an attractive contrast to the black sand. You can take a piece of glacier ice for a refreshing drink.

25 _ The Blue Whale Skeleton
As big as it gets

Jaw bones as long as a medium-sized car, a skull the size of a sofa. Since 2016, a skeleton of the world's largest mammal has been the most remarkable exhibit at the Whale Museum in Húsavík. 'This blue whale more than 20 metres long was stranded on the coast of the Skagi peninsula in 2010. That's an extremely rare event,' says the museum director, Jan Aksel Harder Klitgaard.

'The last time a blue whale was stranded in Iceland was more than 35 years ago. I guess not many more than 10 of them are on display in the whole world.' Other huge whale skeletons, some of them hanging from the museum's roof structure, also convey to visitors a good impression of these remarkable marine mammals, some of which can dive to depths of as much as 3,000 metres.

At present, the population of humpback whales in the North Atlantic is estimated to be about 11,000. This might seem like a large number, but it should not distract attention from the fact that many other species are at acute risk of becoming extinct. Low rates of reproduction, high mortality rates for new-born whales, intensive hunting and increasing environmental threats have resulted in a global reduction of whale populations.

The Whale Museum in Húsavík, one of the most popular whale-watching stations in the whole country, has been educating its public about whales, their habitats and the threats to them since 1997. What started out as a small exhibition quickly grew to become a museum that is today more than 1,600 square metres in size. Its home is a macabre place: a former slaughterhouse. In addition to the skeleton of the blue whale, the museum boasts a further highlight: from October to April it is home to what is presumably the world's most northerly 18-hole putting course. Visitors to the museum can take a putter and play their way through the exhibition from one hole to the next.

Address Hafnarstétt 1, 640 Húsavík | **Getting there** Ring Road 1 heading north, then on route 85 or 87 to Húsavík. The museum is on the left on the main road. | **Hours** May–Sept daily 8.30am–6.30pm, Oct–Dec & Mar–Apr Mon–Fri 9am–2pm | **Tip** About 100 metres further on the road into town, a stone plaque commemorates the training of astronauts for the American Apollo mission. In 1965 and 1967, 32 astronauts, including the famous Neil Armstrong, went to Iceland to train for their moon mission in the bleak stony deserts.

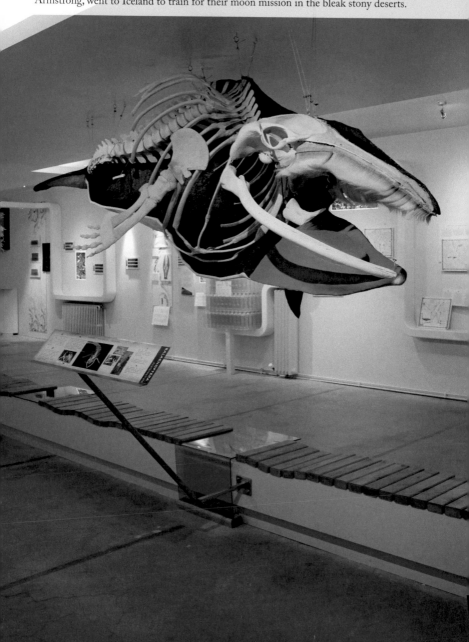

26___Kísilvegur
An upland roller-coaster ride

Apart from a few gentle curves, route 87, called Kísilvegur, passes straight as a die through the hilly landscape between Húsavík and Lake Mývatn. Driving at a brisk speed, on this asphalted road and dirt track you feel you are on a roller-coaster as you zoom up the approach to humps, cross the top and roll down the other side, only to face the next rise a short distance ahead.

Although the altitude is only 300 to 400 metres above sea level, about four kilometres north of Ring Road 1 you get the feeling of being in the uplands. Here, at the end of Kísilvegur, which was built in the late 1960s, you cross a sandy desert, measuring about 130 square kilometres, named Hólasandur. The dominant colour on its slopes of sand, scree and clay is brown, with just a glimpse of green here and there.

Hólasandur probably originated around the year 1700 and spread further and further in the following decades. At that time the area was covered by birch woods and fertile meadows, but overexploitation of the soil led to small areas of wilderness and mud around Lake Sandvatn. Strong south-west winds quickly extended the build-up of sand to the north. The first attempts to stop the expansion of this desert were made in 1965, but it was not until 30 years later that private and state organisations combined with the landowners to put an end to the erosion of earth. Grasses, lupins, woolly willow and birch were planted in many places on Hólasandur. A fence was built around its huge perimeter to keep sheep from eating the young plants. Hólasandur is still far from being a blossoming landscape, but some plants can be seen. If they succeed in withstanding the sand and wind, then in a few decades the roller-coaster journey on Kísilvegur – which means 'gravel path' – will cross green hills instead of brown ones.

Address Kísilvegur, 641 Húsavík | Getting there Ring Road 1 towards Reykjahlíð | Tip At Langavatn route 853 forks off to Grenjaðarstaður. This old farm dates from the age of the Icelandic settlements. A house of turf sods, 775 square metres in size, built in 1865 in the original manner, can be visited there (June to 15 Sept daily 10am–6pm).

27 — Hvítserkur
Well-dressed and petrified

If you are sensitive to sunlight, the answer is to rub in sunscreen or avoid the sun's rays. This applies especially to trolls – it is well known that they are turned to stone in daylight. As a result of this circumstance, in Iceland many stories about trolls are associated with mysterious rock formations which, with a little imagination, can be found to resemble strange creatures. An example of this is the following tale, connected with a 15-metre-high rock named Hvítserkur on the Vatnsnes peninsula.

Many years ago, a large troll lived with his family on the mountain Bæjarfell. One night he was awakened by the tolling of a bell, and quickly realised that this sound could only come from the Þingeyrar monastery. He resolved to destroy the bell once and for all so that he could live in peace and quiet again.

The troll set off for the monastery and had almost reached his destination shortly before dawn broke. Although he was endangered by the approach of daylight, he was determined to destroy the bell. However, before he could do this, the first rays of sunshine appeared over the horizon and turned him to stone. Since that day he has stood in the water off the shore and served as a nesting place for sea birds. It is said that these birds, in their thousands, have given the rock its name over the course of a long period by carelessly depositing their droppings on it. Hvítserkur can be translated as 'white shirt'. It will be a long time before the petrified troll ever takes off the garment.

The sea has given his 'legs' a thorough battering, washing out more and more of the stone from the arches at the foot of the rock. Some time ago it was reinforced with concrete, enabling visitors in future years to exercise their imagination and make up their minds whether Hvítserkur is a troll turned to stone or simply a rock covered by bird droppings.

Address Vatnsnesvegur, 531 Hvammstangi | Getting there Ring Road 1 to the turning onto route 711 towards Vatnsnes. Hvítserkur is on the right after 30 kilometres | Tip On the west side of the Vatnsnes peninsula, about 22 kilometres away, is a farm close to the coast, where a colony of seals lives. A walking trail passes through an area where birds nest (binoculars are available there).

28 Seljavallalaug

A slippery pool by Eyjafjallajökull

Pay at the desk, pass through the turnstile and head for the changing rooms. No – going for a swim in the Seljavallalaug open-air pool is not as simple and convenient as this. Before you leap into the water, you have to master an easy climb in the mountains at the foot of the Eyjafjallajökull volcano. The climb starts at the end of the Seljavellir road, where a path leads from the car park along the Laugará stream into a narrow valley. After some 20 minutes you arrive at the pool. It nestles into the wall of rock that forms one side of the pool. Next to it stands a weather-beaten concrete hut that serves as a changing room. Don't bother to look for showers at Seljavallalaug, and when things are quiet a few birds will use the pool to take a refreshing dip. Nevertheless, the water quality ought not to be too bad, as continuous replenishment from a nearby thermal spring ensures that the pool water is permanently renewed. The bathtub temperature of the water does, however, cause slippery algae to grow, and to lend a greenish hue to the pool.

Seljavallalaug is definitely no longer one of Iceland's secrets for insiders, but it is well worth making the trip. The view of the surrounding mountains is wonderful in almost all weathers, and you feel small and insignificant when bathing between high rock walls.

In spring 1923 a local society, Ungmennafélagið Eyfellingur, built the pool so that residents of the area could learn to swim. It is thought to be Iceland's oldest pool, and with a length of about 25 metres was once one of the largest in the country.

After the eruption of Eyjafjallajökull in 2010, enjoying a swim in the mountains was out of the question. The pool was filled to the brim with ashes, and had to be cleared out again with excavators and hard shovelling. Until the next eruption, the only obstacle to taking a bath at the foot of the volcano is the climb.

Address Seljavellir, 861 Hvolsvöllur | Getting there Ring Road 1, turn onto route 242, which continues as route 2311, and after 1.5 kilometres turn right at the fork to reach the car park. Seljavallalaug is about 43 kilometres south-east of Hvolsvöllur | Hours Always open | Tip A little way west of Seljavallalaug there is a small lay-by on the Ring Road with information about the eruption of Eyjafjallajökull. From here you can see Þorvaldseyri farm, which was severely affected by the disaster. Further west is the Eyjafjallajökull visitor centre.

29 __ Saltverk

Carbon-neutral salt in the old tradition

It's hot in the boiling house of Saltverk on the Reykjanes peninsula in the Westfjords. In three salt-boiling pans with a total volume of 15,500 litres the brine steams away, evaporating to form salt crystals.

While he was a student, Björn Steinar Jónsson and two friends hit upon the idea of extracting salt from sea water, using solely carbon-neutral geothermal energy. This method is not new. As long ago as the 18th century, King Christian VII of Denmark had a salt works built on the same site. 'The Danish connection still exists today. Björn is based in Copenhagen, where he does the international marketing of Saltverk salt, which is in high demand,' says Jón Pálsson. He is Björn's father, and looks after the salt works on Reykjanes. He used to run a construction company, but in 2011 during the financial crisis he joined his son's firm, as the young founders of Saltverk parted at about the same time as a result of divergent interests. Father and son jointly developed the production facility. Sea water is pumped into five pre-heating pans with a combined volume of 400,000 litres, where a pipe filled with geothermally heated water at a temperature of 93 degrees Celsius performs the first evaporation. When the salt content has reached approximately 20 per cent, the concentrated brine flows into the pans in the boiling house. Here the process of evaporation is continued until flakes of salt are formed. These are then 'harvested' manually. The whole process, including drying and packaging, takes about three weeks.

With its carbon-neutral sea salt, Saltverk has become a success in the market for food products. By the end of 2015 the company was supplying 1,400 restaurants, shops and dealers – many with flavoured salts, such as lava and Arctic thyme. Moreover, Björn Steinar Jónsson and his father have revived an old profession in Iceland: the craft of the salt maker.

Address Djúpvegur, about 130 kilometres south-east of 401 Ísafjörður | **Getting there** From Hólmavík take route 61, following the road for 88 kilometres towards Ísafjörður, then turning right on Reykjanes onto route 634 | **Hours** Visible from outside only; when the salt makers have time, they are happy to show visitors the salt pans | **Tip** Continue on route 61 to the Westfjords, passing Litli Baer, a small farm built in 1895, after some 60 kilometres. One kilometre further is a good spot for watching the seals sunbathe.

30_ The Kirkjugólf
A church floor that never was

Every tiler or paver would probably have earned high praise for the 'church floor' of Kirkjugólf. Evenly laid, but with a few natural irregularities in its 80 square metres, this stone surface lies on a grassy area north of the village of Kirkjubæjarklaustur.

The Kirkjugólf consists of the top ends of ancient columns of basalt that project from the ground. They were made more than 9,000 years ago by volcanic activity when magma emerged from the earth at a temperature of more than 1,000 degrees Celsius. The mass of lava cooled, contracted and formed cracks, which extended from the cooled surface down to the warm interior of the lava. This process created the shape of the basalt columns, which are often six-sided. In the course of millennia, the 'church floor' was scoured smooth by waves and glaciers. Manual work played no part. Since 1987 the Kirkjugólf has been a protected natural monument, and although the Icelandic word for 'church' is part of its name, it is not thought that a place of worship ever stood on the basalt surface.

Nevertheless, Kirkjubæjarklaustur possesses a famous church. It stood approximately on the site of the present-day chapel. Here Pastor Jón Steingrímsson is said to have held his famous 'fire mass' on 20 July, 1783. At that time, a stream of lava from the great volcanic eruption of Laki was threatening the inhabitants of Kirkjubæjarklaustur and the area. Knowing that this could be the last church service that they would celebrate together, the pastor delivered a passionate sermon, and the congregation prayed for salvation. A short time later, what seemed like a miracle happened: the stream of lava stopped just short of Kirkjubæjarklaustur. With divine help, Jón Steingrímsson had seemingly saved his people. But only briefly: the eight-month eruption of Laki caused the deaths of tens of thousands, in Iceland and over the whole world.

Address Geirland, 880 Kirkjubæjarklaustur | Getting there Ring Road 1, turning into the road Geirland at the roundabout | Tip In the old cemetery at Kirkjubæjarklaustur is the grave of the famous pastor, Jón Steingrímsson, and his wife. Some ruins of the old church can also be seen.

31 Systrafoss

Not a good place for sisters

In some places it flows, elsewhere it falls down the steep wall of rock: Systrafoss, the 'waterfall of the sisters'. At the foot of the falls, nothing reveals what awaits on the plateau above the village. Those who make the effort and ascend along the quietly splashing waterfalls will have their breath taken away twice over – first by the steepness of the climb, and then by the spectacular view of Kirkjubæjarklaustur and the 50-square-kilometre lava field of Landbrótsholar.

Inland, embedded in green meadows and the gentle hills of the plateau, lies Systravatn, the 'sisters' lake'. In the late 12th century it was a popular place to swim for the inhabitants of the nunnery in Kirkjubæjarklaustur. Its name derives from the story that two nuns once disappeared here. According to the legend, one day the sisters saw a hand rising from the water with a golden comb (in other versions it was a golden ring). When they reached to take it, the hand pulled them into the water, and they were never seen again. The way the tale is told by the Icelandic author Jón Árnason is even more mysterious. In his story, after the first nun vanished into the lake, a large, stone-grey horse appeared to the second woman. She mounted it and rode into the water to get the golden comb. Afterwards no one ever set eyes on either the nuns or the horse or the comb. Since then the lake has borne the name Systravatn, and the waterfall has been called Systrafoss.

Is this pure invention, or is there any truth to the tale? It has been shown that between 1186 and 1554 a nunnery stood in Kirkjubæjarklaustur, not far from the waterfall. Excavations of the site have demonstrated this.

The remains of a loom and what are probably the oldest knitting needles in Iceland were found in the dig. Back in the Middle Ages, Icelanders already seem to have been keen on knitting and weaving.

Address Klausturvegur, 880 Kirkjubæjarklaustur | **Getting there** Ring Road 1, at Kirkjubæjarklaustur turn off onto Klausturvegur | **Tip** The name of the 'sisters' rock' Systrastapi west of Kirkjubæjarklaustur also derives from two sinful nuns. The story says that they were burned at the stake and buried on Systrastapi. After the Reformation, one of the nuns was declared innocent. Since then, it is said, flowers have grown on her side of the grave.

32 Hvalfjörður

Down below, or all the way round?

On the Ring Road heading north, about four kilometres past the village of Grundarhverfi, drivers have to make up their minds whether to go down or around. If you pay the toll to take the 5,762-metre concrete tunnel beneath Hvalfjörður, you will reach your destination more quickly, but you will also miss something quite special. The detour of almost 60 kilometres around the fjord passes through some unbelievably lovely scenery.

Ever since Iceland was first populated by humans, people have settled on the shores of Hvalfjörður, and in the 14th century Maríuhöfn on the south side of the fjord was one of the island's foremost trading posts. The deep sea channel was suitable for large ships that brought foodstuffs and other goods to Iceland. Today, cargo ships anchor on the north side, where the industrial harbour of Grundartangi and the Norðurál aluminium smelting plant are located. This area is a small blot on what is otherwise beautiful countryside.

Where the steep slopes of the surrounding mountains do not rise right by the water's edge, grass-covered hills form the banks of the fjord. Sheep graze here between large rocks that have broken off from the rock walls and rolled down the mountainside. On the horizon, snow-capped peaks can sometimes be seen, and in the middle of the fjord are small islands, habitats for various kinds of birds.

During World War II, the south side of Hvalfjörður was an important base for both the British and the American navy. Freight ships gathered in the fjord and formed convoys to undertake the voyage to Russia, escorted by warships. At the end of the war, the armed forces left Hvalfjörður. Only the remains of the British base in Hvítanes serve as a reminder of those days – and the American landing stage on the north side, which is now used, for purposes that are no more peaceful, by a whaling station.

Address Hvalfjarðarvegur, 276 Kjósarhreppur | Getting there Ring Road 1 towards Akranes, then route 47 | Tip Approximately at the end of Hvalfjörður lies a car park for walkers. The trail leads to Glymur, one of the highest waterfalls in Iceland. Take good boots, as there are some steep bits of climbing on the route. The view across Hvalfjörður is breathtaking.

33 Jökulsárgljúfur
A deep drop into a glacial ravine

The 24-kilometre-long ravine Jökulsárgljúfur is one of the most impressive in all of Iceland. In the course of centuries it was carved out of the rock, probably by enormous glaciers and the river Jökulsá á Fjöllum. Iceland's second-longest watercourse, with a length of 206 kilometres, transports its grey-brown masses of water across the country. It rises on the northern glacier of Vatnajökull, grows through the addition of melt water in the highlands, and swells further on its way to the sea as tributaries flow in. In summer it carries up to 23,000 tonnes of sediment per day – the equivalent of the load of 575 40-ton trucks.

These unbelievable quantities of water, sand and rubble not only power through the Jökulsárgljúfur gorge, which is up to 100 metres deep and in places 500 metres wide, but also pour over several waterfalls. The most imposing of the falls is undoubtedly Dettifoss – 'the plunging waterfall'. The art of creative name-giving seems to have been defeated in this case. On the other hand, something as naturally impressive as this has no need of a spectacular name. With a drop of 45 metres and a roaring sound to match, Dettifoss forms the upper end of Jökulsárgljúfur. In summer, approximately 400,000 litres of water per second flow over it and into the ravine – much more when the river is in spate.

One of Europe's biggest waterfalls ceaselessly sends fine spray into the sky. Most of the droplets land on the more densely vegetated west side of Jökulsárgljúfur. This may be a blessing to the plant life of this barren area, but for photographers it is a curse, as the fine drops coat their lenses. For this reason the east side of the gorge is a better place for taking snapshots. Not far away, upriver and downriver, are two more waterfalls: Selfoss, not high with its 10-metre drop but wide, and the 27-metre-high Hafragilsfoss.

Address Hólsfjallavegur (east side), Dettifossvegur (west side), about 70 kilometres south of 671 Kópasker | Getting there Ring Road 1, turning off on route 862 to the west side or route 864 for the east side | Tip The car park on the east side of Dettifoss is the starting point for three walking trails of varying degrees of difficulty. They are between 1.5 and 9 kilometres long, and lead along the gorge to all three waterfalls.

34__The Kópavogskirkja
A church, opera or fast-food restaurant?

The white Kópavogskirkja stands majestically on the Borgarholt. This hill of lava was created at the end of the last ice age, about 10,000 years ago, and has been a protected natural monument since 1981. For this reason, the area surrounding the church has not been built up, and commands a far-reaching view across Kópavogura and Garðabær, and as far as Reykjavík.

In designing the church, the architects departed from traditional styles. The building consists of a nave and transept that, seen from the air, form a cross with arms of equal length. The exterior of the Kópavogskirkja is characterised by its parabolic arches, which, with a little imagination, are reminiscent either of the Sydney Opera House or the logo of a chain of hamburger restaurants. But Pastor Sigurður Arnarson does not appreciate the nickname 'McDonald's church'. 'In Kópavogur not many people say this, as they have memories associated with the church. But of course there are a few jokers who use this nickname.' The town's coat of arms also contains the striking arches, underlining the importance of the Kópavogskirkja, the first church in the town and the only one until 1994.

During the four-year construction period up to 1958, the church was fitted with stained-glass windows, designed by the Icelandic artist Gerður Helgadóttir. They were installed by a glass company called Oidtmann (not related to the author) from Linnich in Germany. The unusual architecture did not allow a bell tower, and the peal of bells had to be set up next to the church. The inhabitants of Kópavogur come up to the Borgarholt for more reasons than church services and prayer. 'Some drive their cars around the church, park for a few minutes, and have a break while enjoying the view,' says Sigurður. 'Especially in spring and summer, when you can see the sun setting over Snæfellsjökull from here.'

Address Hamraborg, 200 Kópavogur, +354 554-1898 | **Getting there** Bus 1, 2, 4, 28 or 35 to Hamraborg; from Reykjavík take route 40 to the exit Kópavogur C, then right at the roundabout | **Hours** During church services or by arrangement | **Tip** In sight of the Kópavogs-skirkja stands the Gerðarsafn Museum. It was opened in 1994 to commemorate the stained-glass artist Gerður Helgadóttir and is Iceland's only museum that was built to honour a woman artist. It also exhibits works by other 20th-century artists, most of them from Iceland.

35__Hverfjall
2,500 years of natural symmetry

Resembling an old heap of coal and visible from a long distance, Hverfjall rises heavenwards on the east bank of the Mývatn. This grey-and-black mountain of rubble in the north of Iceland was not, however, raised by human agency but created more than 2,500 years ago as a result of volcanic activity. It is part of the Krafla volcanic system. Scientific investigations concluded that hot magma encountered ground water, generating a cloud of steam that hurled huge masses of rock into the air with unimaginable force. Around the column of steam, fragments of rock fell to earth and piled up to form Hverfjall. At the edge of the crater the mountain has a diameter of about one kilometre, at its foot twice as much. Its slopes are between 80 and 170 metres high. This difference might derive from the direction of the wind during the eruption, causing more rubble to land on the south side. There are only a few craters of this kind with such a regular structure in the whole world, which is why Hverfjall was given protection as a nature reserve in 2011.

In summer, the green vegetation on the banks of the Mývatn makes an interesting contrast to the lack of colour in the crater. Two walking trails lead up to it. The easier one starts from the car park to the north-west of Hverfjall. Depending on your level of fitness, the ascent to the edge of the crater will take between 10 and 20 minutes. When you reach the top, a stunning view opens up across the Mývatn, and in the distance you can see steam rising from hot springs. The interior of Hverfjall is also an impressive sight, although less spectacular. To walk all round the edge of the crater, a distance of 3.2 kilometres, will take you about one hour. In order to preserve the unique formation of Hverfjall from damage, it is strictly forbidden to leave the walking trails or to descend into the crater.

Address Route 8816, 660 Mývatn | Getting there Ring Road 1 to Reykjahlíð, then turn off onto route 848. After 3.5 kilometres, Hverfjall is on the left | Tip Grjótagjá lies a few kilometres north of Hverfjall on route 860. This small lava cave contains a geothermal spring and was once a popular place to bathe. Since a volcanic eruption close to Krafla, the water temperature has risen and bathing is prohibited, partly because of the danger of falling rocks. However, the entrance to the cave can be visited.

36 — The Mývatn Natural Baths
The Blue Lagoon's little sisters

The natural baths of Mývatn steam milky-blue. They lie in the north-east of Iceland and offer geothermal relaxation and a pleasant bath to many travellers to Iceland who feel worn down by their outdoor activities. Although the tradition of bathing in hot springs goes back decades in this region, the baths at Mývatn do not in fact have a natural origin. These man-made constructions are filled with water from a borehole 2,500 metres deep in Bjarnarflag, which also supplies the geothermal power station there – the smallest power plant operated by the state energy utility Landsvirkjun. Including the neighbouring pools, into which water flows at a temperature of 130 degrees Celsius and is cooled to a pleasant 36 to 40 degrees, the lagoon has a volume of about 3.5 million litres.

Since summer 2004 the baths at Mývatn have been rivals to their big sister, the world-famous 'blue lagoon' close to Keflavík airport, giving visitors a fun place to bathe with a fantastic view of the surrounding mountains. They lie a little way off the main tourist track, even though they are no longer a scene of undisturbed solitude.

The water of these springs, alkaline and rich in minerals, is said to be beneficial in cases of asthma and other respiratory complaints, while the minerals in the lagoon are reported to alleviate skin problems. The slightly rotten smell has nothing to do with poor water quality, of course, but is a result of the sulphur content of the geothermal water, which is somewhat higher at Mývatn than in other parts of Iceland. The chemical properties of the geothermal water eliminate any undesirable bacteria in the lagoon, and make it unnecessary to add chlorine or any other chemicals. Of course it does not obviate the need to take a shower before entering the bath. By the way – in Iceland it is usual to shower naked, and only then to put on swimwear.

Address Jarðbaðshólar, 660 Mývatn | **Getting there** Ring Road 1 from Reykjahlíð towards Egilsstaðir, turn right 500 metres after the fork onto route 860 | **Hours** June–Aug daily 9am–midnight, Sept–May daily noon–10pm, different times at Christmas and New Year | **Tip** Opposite the approach road to the Mývatn baths stands the Bjarnarflag power station. It uses the steam from the geothermal region at the nearby Námafjall mountain to generate electricity. It has been in operation since 1969, produces three megawatts and was the first power station of its kind in Iceland.

37__Námafjall
Boiling mud and rotten eggs

Around Námafjall, close to Lake Mývatn, the earth steams and bubbles. The mountain is part of the great Krafla volcanic system, which extends across the country for almost 100 kilometres in a north-south direction. To the east of Námafjall lies the Hverir high-temperature zone with its many steam vents and mud springs. Here the ground is coloured blue, grey, orange, yellow and white. From some distance you can see the evil-smelling clouds rising, and the closer you get, the more intensely it stinks of rotten eggs. Gases containing hydrogen sulphide are the reason for this. They are created when cold groundwater penetrates deep into the earth through cracks and crevices, meets hot magma, evaporates and comes back to the surface. On its way back, the water vapour carries with it the stinking gases that emerge on Námafjall from solfataras and fumaroles. These are the names for places where steam is emitted, usually at temperatures above 100 degrees Celsius. The sulphur is mostly deposited around the edges of the solfataras and fumaroles, colouring the rock.

In addition to these steaming holes in the ground, in the Hverir high-temperature zone there are many seething mud holes. These are hot springs with low quantities of water, from which gases containing hydrogen sulphide also come to the earth's surface. When mixed with water they form sulphuric acid and gradually transform the rocky ground into viscous mud.

Because nobody knows exactly where the ground has been affected by these emissions, you should keep strictly to the marked walking trails that pass through the area and go up the mountain. Contact with hot mud can lead to serious burns. If you pay attention to this warning, you will be rewarded with a wonderful view across the whole Mývatn region from the summit of Námafjall and get a close-up experience of Iceland's living geology.

Address Þjóðvegur, 660 Mývatn | Getting there Ring Road 1 towards Lake Mývatn; Námafjall is about 5.5 kilometres east of Reykjahlíð | Tip Near Námafjall, route 863 leads to the Krafla geothermal power station. About 4.5 kilometres beyond the turn-off, you pass a shower on the hard shoulder on the right. Its purpose is unknown. It is well worth visiting the region around the volcano Krafla, a few kilometres further on.

38__Sigurgeir's Bird Museum
Living for birds

Sigurgeir Stefánsson never lived to see the bird museum that bears his name. The exhibition consisting of more than 300 items is his legacy. When he died in a tragic accident in 1999 he was 37 years old and at work on Lake Mývatn. With two colleagues he was trying to repair an underwater telephone cable. A strong wind caused their boat to capsize and the three men fell into the cold water. Sigurgeir was the only one wearing a life jacket and was rescued, but later died of hypothermia. His two companions drowned. After Sigurgeir's sudden death, his family fulfilled his greatest wish: with donations from friends and local people, they built a museum for his collection of birds.

At the age of 20 Sigurgeir had begun to collect and stuff birds. However, no animal died in the pursuit of this activity. He never went hunting, but his hobby was well known in the area, and Sigurgeir was informed whenever anybody found a dead bird. The collection grew to the point where he exhibited it in a small hut and admitted visitors.

The present bird museum was opened in 2008. It contains a total of 14 glass cases filled with stuffed birds, and is owned by the family. The dimly lit circular exhibition space looks like a hall of mirrors. Everywhere birds are perched with their dead eyes. They are reflected in the glass of the showcases and disappear again when you move on. The chirping of birds, the call of eagles and the quacking of ducks from a loudspeaker fill the room with life. This is the same acoustic background that can be clearly heard around the museum in summer, when countless swarms of midges hover above the lake and provide abundant food for both fish and birds. It is hardly surprising that more than 40 species of birds nest on Lake Mývatn. The site was well chosen, and Sigurgeir himself could scarcely have found a better location for his museum.

Address Ytri-Neslönd, 660 Mývatn | **Getting there** Ring Road 1 from Reykjahlíð heading north-west; at the junction with route 87 continue left on the Ring Road, and after 2.9 kilometres turn left to the museum | **Hours** Daily 15 May–31 May & 25 Aug–31 Oct noon–5pm, 1 June–24 Aug 9am–6pm, 1 Nov–14 May 2–4pm | **Tip** Vindbelgjarfjall, a 530-metre-high mountain of volcanic origin, lies to the west of the museum, accessed on Ring Road 1 heading south. A walking trail about 2.5 kilometres long leads up it for a fantastic panoramic view.

39__The Ski Jump
Telemark by the village pond

Bergisel, Holmenkollen and Schattenberg – these are the names of three ski jumps that are all an integral part of the history of international competitions in this sport. The hill in Ólafsfjörður called Gullatún ranks much further down this list of major venues, but for ski jumping in Iceland it is no less important than the others. In summer 1967 work commenced on the small concrete ski jump, which is perhaps 15 metres long – the only such structure existing in Iceland. A year later it had been completed, built entirely by volunteers, as was normal in those days when constructing sports facilities.

For lovers of ski jumping this was a big improvement. Before it was built, they had spent most of the available time piling up a ramp by hand rather than actually training, as K. Haraldur Gunnlaugsson from the local Rotary Club recalls. The new facilities for training and competitions soon paid off. In the years that followed, many ski jumpers from Ólafsfjörður and its region were successful in national competitions and championships. In the early 1990s, interest in ski jumping gradually declined, and the last ski jumping competition in Iceland was held in 1995. Since then the concrete ramp has only been used for having fun. On 17 June, the national holiday to celebrate the foundation of the state of Iceland, the people of Ólafsfjörður like to turn their little ski jump into a water slide. Special sheets of plastic are then laid on the approach and on the platform, and sprayed with water. All who are brave enough can then slide down – an experience every bit as adventurous as ski jumping.

The citizens of Ólafsfjörður are proud of their ski jump, which is bang in the centre of town and forms a kind of landmark between the houses, village pond and swimming pool. 'And to make sure it stays that way, we regularly give it a fresh coat of paint,' says Haraldur.

Address Corner of Aðalgata and Ólafsvegur, 625 Ólafsfjörður | **Getting there** From Akureyri on route 82, in Ólafsfjörður straight ahead until you see the ski jump on the left on a slope above the campsite | **Tip** Take a walk around the nearby lake called Ólafsfjarðarvatn. Its shore is at the edge of the village, and it is known for having many species of fish: depending on the tides, salt water from the fjord flows into the lake, creating different layers of water in which both freshwater and saltwater fish can live.

40___The Bridge Pier

Like matchsticks in a sandpit

When 50,000 cubic metres of water per second rush towards the sea, sweeping huge blocks of ice weighing up to 2,000 tonnes with them, nothing made by humans can stand up to the force of nature.

This is impressively demonstrated by the buckled bridge piers that stand on the eastern edge of the Skeiðarársandur alluvial plain as a kind of admonition. They recall the devastating glacial burst that began on 5 November, 1996. A volcanic eruption had taken place beneath the northern part of the Vatnajökull glacier. In consequence, huge quantities of melt water were released. They gathered in Lake Grímsvötn, which is situated beneath the glacier. When the water pressure became too great, the barriers of ice shattered and a flood wave moved towards the sea with violent force.

When the glacial burst subsided after about two days, the extent of the destruction could be seen. Many roads and dams had been simply swept away by the masses of water. A 376-metre-long bridge over the river Gígukvísl had disappeared completely, and 176 metres of road over the Skeiðará plain were so severely damaged that repair work was not completed until summer 1998.

The first road across the Skeiðarársandur had not been built until the early 1970s. Before that, people had to undertake perilous tours over the glacier or cross the glacial rivers with specially equipped cars. This meant that the region to the east of the sandy plain was isolated until that time. With a surface area of more than 1,000 square kilometres, the Skeiðarársandur plain is Iceland's most extensive alluvial landscape. When you drive across it on the Ring Road, you encounter little in the way of vegetation. Apart from a few kinds of grass, almost nothing grows in the grey-black glacial sand. The upside of this is that you can confidently drive a good 27 kilometres without fear of running over a sheep.

Address Þjóðvegur, 785 Öræfi | **Getting there** Ring Road 1, 67 kilometres east of Kirkjubæjarklaustur | **Tip** About 5 kilometres to the north, the Skaftafell visitor centre has an exhibition about the glaciers and volcanoes of the region. Items found after a fatal expedition by British students in 1952–53 are on display. Two participants were never found, and part of their equipment was located in 2006 on Skaftafellsjökull.

41 The Látrabjarg Rock
Sea-bird city

At the tip of the Látrabjarg peninsula there is a pungent smell in the air, like that in a bird's cage. No birds are confined here, however. Ten different species of sea birds nest on the cliffs, which are up to 440 metres high, and during daylight hours the traffic levels here are reminiscent of an urban highway in the rush hour. Seemingly without a moment's break, the birds fly out over the sea or return to Iceland's most populous bird rock with food in their beaks. Along the 14 kilometres of this stretch of coast, which includes the Látrabjarg peninsula, guillemots, razorbills, fulmars, kittiwakes and of course puffins have found a home. Látrabjarg is especially good as a place to watch the gaudy-beaked puffin, Iceland's national bird. They live in little tunnels that they dig into the soft earth at the brink of the cliffs and sit there, as if posing for a photo, before setting off again to hunt small fish.

If you go there, don't try to get too close to the cliff edge. For one thing this disturbs the birds, for another you would be putting your life at risk. Signs have been placed everywhere to warn visitors of the danger of falling as a result of strong gusts of wind or tripping on the uneven, hollowed-out ground.

In the past, too, Látrabjarg was a hazardous place. Farmers suffered injuries while collecting birds' eggs on the cliffs, and ships ran aground on the rocks. On 12 December, 1947 the British trawler *Dhoon* suffered this fate. In a rescue operation that lasted three days, the farmers of Látrabjarg saved 12 seamen by descending the cliffs on ropes and bringing the trawler crew back up by the same means. A year later, while a documentary film was being made about the wreck of the *Dhoon*, a second shipwreck happened. The film maker Óskar Gíslason recorded the events with his camera, and later used these scenes as part of the film.

Address Örlygshafnarvegur, 60 kilometres south-west of 451 Patreksfjörður | **Getting there** Coming from Flókalundur take route 62, then turn left onto route 612 and follow the road for 46 kilometres | **Tip** Egill Ólafsson's folk museum lies 23 kilometres from Látrabjarg on route 612. You can't miss it, because two small ships stand high and dry in front of the building, together with parts of a US Navy aircraft.

42 Rauðasandur
The feeling of the South Seas

Not many visitors to Iceland bring a beach towel and parasol with them: with an average temperature of about 13 degrees Celsius, the Icelandic summer is simply not suitable for a beach holiday. Despite this, the beach at Rauðasandur was given a place in the top rankings of an American budget-flight internet site in 2014, in the category 'the most beautiful inaccessible beaches'. This is definitely justified in the case of Rauðasandur. Before you can trail your feet through the sand of this beach, which is about 10 kilometres long, you have to undergo an adventurous road trip. When you leave the main road to approach Rauðasandur, you will have sweaty palms unless you are used to off-road driving. Around steep, narrow hairpin bends on a potholed gravel surface, you wind your way down into the valley. On one side are rocks, on the other an abyss. Safety rails? Forget it! But when you have made it through this part of the journey, on the last of the bends you will already be rewarded by a wonderful view of the beach.

Rauðasandur means 'red sand', even though the colour is more like golden yellow. Shells that are not present in other parts of Iceland produce the colour, making a welcome change from the usual black lava beaches. Very few visitors venture into the cold water, and most people only come to Rauðasandur for a long walk. The beach seems to be an endless expanse, especially at low tide. It is all the more idyllic for the sheep that graze at the edge of the sand and only move away if you get too close to them.

Rauðasandur is not the only beach of light-coloured sand in Iceland. Those who travel around the Westfjords will discover a whole series of little bays where you can imagine a little South Sea atmosphere when the weather is good. At the first contact with the water, however, this immediately gives way to a North Atlantic feeling.

Address Rauðasandsvegur, about 32 kilometres south of 451 Patreksfjörður | Getting there Coming from Flókalundur on route 62, turn left onto route 612, then left again after 7.5 kilometres onto route 614 | Tip Immediately behind the beach is a black wooden church, the Saurbæjarkirkja. It was built in Reykhólar between 1855 and 1859, stood there until 1975 and was re-erected by the Rauðasandur beach, where it is surrounded by a small cemetery and a stone wall.

43__The Arctic Henge
A visionary stone formation to attract tourists

Rough blocks of stone form the four heavenly gates of the Arctic Henge. In the middle is a monument consisting of columns 11 metres high that touch at their tips. They stand on a hill above the little town of Raufarhöfn in the north-east of Iceland and are part of Erlingur Thoroddsen's master plan for tourism. He is a hotel owner who has been thinking for many years about the details of his Arctic Henge, which is intended to attract more visitors. One day the heavenly gates are to be linked with a stone wall, making a ring with a diameter of 50 metres around the site. Inside this will be a second ring consisting of 68 stones and four large sculptures. On the model of the signs of the zodiac, each stone in the ring will stand for part of the year and will be allocated a dwarf from the Völuspá, a famous medieval Nordic poem.

This relates to Erlingur's marketing strategy. 'All visitors can identify with a dwarf, according to their date of birth. We will also sell a souvenir for every dwarf.' His plan is that these souvenirs will be made by people from Raufarhöfn. 'Nothing made in China, only Icelandic handicrafts,' says Erlingur. 'This means that everyone can contribute to the project and benefit from it.'

Although the Arctic Henge is still far from completion, the bright nights of midsummer are already the best time for a visit. 'It is a magical experience when the setting sun shines through the north gate,' comments Erlingur enthusiastically. In his imagination, he pictures this view on postcards of Raufarhöfn.

As the association that is responsible for the Arctic Henge often lacks money for materials and machines, the construction work has dragged on since 2004. When will the Arctic Henge be completed? Erlingur gives an optimistic answer to the question. 'It doesn't matter when – the important thing is that it gets finished.'

Address On route 870, 675 Raufarhöfn | Getting there Take route 85 to Raufarhöfn, pass through and go straight ahead on route 870 to the henge on the left just beyond the village | Hours Always open | Tip Route 870 leads to Iceland's most northerly point (apart from Grímsey Island). The Hraunhafnartangi lighthouse stands here, a few hundred metres south of the Arctic Circle in an area where many sea birds breed.

44__ The Shelters

Basic emergency accommodation

Most of them are orange-red. They are either made from wood, or are plastic capsules that look like space ships. These shelters run by Slysavarnafélagið Landsbjörg, the Icelandic Search and Rescue Association, are anchored to the ground with cables so that the wind does not blow them away. Most of them are in the uplands, in lonely coastal regions and on little-used mountain passes: in all those places where Iceland's notorious weather can strike with special violence. The shelters, which are visible from far away, provide protection for anyone who gets into a hazardous situation. In 2014 alone the members of Slysavarnafélagið Landsbjörg set out 1,400 times on rescue missions.

In the age of smartphones and good network coverage, the shelters may have lost some of their importance, because it is now much easier to call for help than in the past. Nevertheless, all those who are in difficulties will feel relieved when they are able to shut the door of a hut behind them to keep out the rain, snow or storm.

The sparse equipment of the shelters includes a radio for sending an SOS, a few bunk beds, a small gas stove and some food supplies that keep for a long time, for example packet soup and rusks. There is usually a guest book among the inventory so that stranded travellers can record their names while they wait for rescue or better weather. It needs to be emphasised that the shelters are not intended as accommodation for tourists who don't feel like putting up their tent.

They are usually maintained by the local rescue teams of Slysavarnafélagið Landsbjörg. Depending on the remoteness of the individual huts, visits from team members may be rare events. Anyone who is curious to take a look inside a shelter should therefore take care to close the door firmly afterwards, so that the hut itself is not affected by weather and ends up needing help.

Address For example: Vestfjarðarvegur on Klettsfjöll, 380 Reykhólahreppur | Getting there Via route 60 to the Westfjords towards Patreksfjörður, then 5 kilometres beyond the turn-off to the F 66 | Hours Always open | Tip 80 kilometres further ontowards Patreksfjörður on route 62, the Birkimelur open-air swimming pool lies at the edge of a large beach and has natural geothermal water.

45 __ The Goat Centre
Saving the Iceland goat

It is almost impossible to travel in Iceland – whether as a driver on the Ring Road, as a walker in the highlands or as a diner in a restaurant – without making the acquaintance of sheep. The Iceland goat is a different matter. If you would like to see a representative of this rare breed, you will have to go and look for one.

On Jóhanna Bergmann Þorvaldsdóttir's farm you have excellent prospects of success, as around 200 of the 900 goats in Iceland live with her in Háafell. About 15 years ago the situation was different. At that time there remained only a handful of Iceland goats, which originally came to the island with the Vikings. Through years of work breeding the race, Jóhanna succeeded in increasing their number, even though it is difficult to market their meat, milk and wool. In recent years the goat farm in Háafell had financial difficulties and was only saved by means of a crowd-funding campaign on the internet. In 2014 people all around the world donated some 100,000 euros in only a few weeks to secure the survival of the farm and its animals. If this campaign had failed, the way ahead for the goats would have led straight to the slaughterhouse, despite the fact that celebrity film stars such as the white billy-goat Casanova were among the animals. He and his herd had their big moment in the fourth series of the fantasy drama *Game of Thrones*, when a fire-breathing dragon attacked the goats.

For the time being the future of the goats seems no longer to be threatened, as construction of a dairy is planned to ensure the financial stability of the farm for the future. A visit to Háafell is especially suitable for children. The goats gambol about in a large meadow where they can pose for photographs or be stroked. Jóhanna and her family are pleased to tell the story of their animals, and in the farm shop you can buy goat products.

Address Háafell on Hvítársíðuvegur, about 18 kilometres north of 320 Reykholt,
+354 845-2331 | Getting there Take Ring Road 1, then turn onto route 50, continue on
route 522 north of Kleppjárnsreykir and then turn right again onto route 523, following
this road for 8 kilometres | Hours June–Aug daily 1–6pm, or by arrangement | Tip Two
beautiful waterfalls lie 14 kilometres to the east. Hraunfossar consists of many small rivulets
that flow out of the lava stone into the river Hvítá. Higher up, the water of Barnafoss
gushes with a loud roar through a narrow rocky gorge.

46 _ Snorri's Bath

The poet's bath, protected heritage

If you dip a finger into the water of the Snorralaug, you can picture in your mind's eye how, in the early 13th century, the famous Icelander Snorri Sturluson sat in a small stone basin, chatting with friends and soothing his weary bones. Looking back from today's perspective, the poet, historian and politician Sturluson thoroughly deserved these moments of leisure. He is regarded as the author of the famous *Snorra-Edda*, a book of history about Nordic mythology and the art of Old Norse poetry. The *Heimskringla*, a history of the Norwegian kings, is also attributed to him.

From 1206 until 1241 Snorri lived and worked in Reykholt, which was then seen as the cultural and political centre of medieval Iceland. His love of bathing is described in several passages of the Sturlunga Saga, a kind of family chronicle. These references gave rise to the present-day name of the Snorralaug, which means 'Snorri's bath'. This basin of calcareous sinter has a diameter of about 4 metres and is 70 to 100 centimetres deep. It is supplied with water through a pipe from a hot spring called Skrifla. The Snorralaug is one of the first archaeological finds in the country, and was given protected status in 1817. Bathing in it is therefore prohibited, of course.

Behind the small wooden door at the side of the pool lies an underground passage that, in Snorri's day, belonged to his house, which lay above. One dark night in autumn 1241, not even this secret escape route could save his life: Gissur Þorvaldsson, who had been sent by King Håkon IV of Norway, murdered Snorri Sturluson in his own house. This event was preceded by an uprising against the king. Håkon IV suspected Snorri of involvement in it. Neither his innocence nor the Heimskringla, the history in which he had perpetuated the memory of the royal houses of Norway, protected him from murder.

Address Hálsasveitarvegur, 320 Reykholt | Getting there From Reykjavík take route 50, going straight ahead onto route 518 just beyond Kleppjárnsreykir and turning left to the car park on the left after 4.9 kilometres | Hours Always open | Tip Above Snorralaug stands the Reykholtskirkja. This lovely old wooden church was built in 1886–87 and is a protected heritage building. It stands right next to the new church, which was consecrated in 1996.

47 __ The Water Pipeline
Hot and shiny

Since the early 1980s, Akranes, Borgarnes and Hvanneyri have had a water pipeline connecting them with the Deildartunguhver thermal spring. The pipes, most of which are underground, have a total length of more than 100 kilometres and are one of the longest geothermal pipelines in Iceland. The hot water streams ceaselessly from Deildartunguhver into the shining silver pipe of the distribution station. From there it reaches the water tanks in Akranes, some 70 kilometres away by car, after about 24 hours. Although most of the pipes are made of asbestos and additionally insulated with mineral wool, on its journey the water loses approximately 20 degrees Celsius, but is still hot enough for you to scald your fingers badly.

At the place where the spring emerges, the message for visitors is: keep your distance! Like a seething saucepan, Deildartunguhver spews steaming water to the surface, and the fountains that bubble out of the ground at the foot of the little hill cannot simply be turned off like the ring on a cooker. It is not recommended to let water at 96 degrees Celsius come into contact with your skin.

Since 1978 Deildartunguhver, close to Reykholt, has been a protected natural monument. It produces up to 180 litres of thermal water per second, which makes it one of the most plentiful hot-water springs in the world. It is part of a low-temperature zone where water is heated by hot rock at a depth of one to three kilometres and comes back to the earth's surface through cracks in the ground. It is thought that the water emerging from Deildartunguhver fell over 1,000 years ago in the highlands as rain or snow.

In addition to the bubbling or steaming springs, when visiting Deildartunguhver take note of the colours and vegetation of the surroundings. Among other plants, the deer fern grows here – a species not found elsewhere in Iceland.

Address Deildartunguhver, 320 Reykholt | **Getting there** From Reykjavík take route 50, turn left just after Kleppjárnsreykir and continue on route 50, turning left to Deildartunguhver after 900 metres | **Tip** At the car park buy a few tomatoes from the greenhouses near Deildartunguhver. A bag costs 200 króna (about 1.50 euros), and the money is placed in a wooden box – have the right change ready!

48__ The Bridge between the Continents

Where Europe and North America are close together

On one side is the Eurasian continental plate, on the other the North American continental plate. They are connected by a steel bridge that is just 18 metres long. To make it clear from the beginning: it is not possible, of course, simply to jump across from one tectonic plate to the other. Nevertheless, the bridge makes it clear that this patch of earth is a place with special characteristics. On the Reykjanes peninsula in the south-west of Iceland the mid-Atlantic ridge, one of the earth's seams, rises from the ocean. This is where the Eurasian and North American continental plates collide. The border runs diagonally through Iceland from south-west to north-east. Geological rift zones of this kind are revealed on the earth's surface only in a few places around the world. Usually they lie deep beneath the sea.

Each year the Eurasian and the North American continental plates drift about two centimetres further apart. For the bridge across the narrow trench, this poses no immediate threat. In this location it serves only as a symbol of the rift between the two continents.

Wherever tectonic plates meet, rumblings beneath the surface occur frequently. Earthquakes create new openings, and the trenches that arise are refilled with rock by means of volcanic eruptions. Over millions of years, tectonic movements like those here on the mid-Atlantic ridge have not only created the continents, but have also raised the highest mountains and opened the deepest ocean trenches on the planet. Foremost among these are the Himalaya range in Nepal, and the Galathea trench in the Pacific, which goes down to a depth of about 10,500 metres. However, it will take a few more million years of tectonic activity before the Reykjanes peninsula and the bridge between the continents reach these dimensions.

Address Nesvegur, 233 Reykjanesbær | Getting there From Reykjavík take route 41 to
Njarðvík, turn left onto route 44 towards Hafnir and continue on route 425 | Tip Further
south on route 425 is the Gunnuhver geothermal area, where steam and volcanic gases rise
from mud springs and fumaroles. Adjacent to the spring is the lovely lighthouse of Reykjanes.

49 __ Rokksafn Íslands

Icelandic music history in Rock City

The music scene is as vibrant in Iceland as anywhere else in the world – mainly, of course, in Reykjavík, the capital city. Rokksafn Íslands, Iceland's museum of rock 'n' roll, is about 45 kilometres away, however, in Keflavík in the district of Reykjanesbær. The exhibition starts off with stars of the 1930s and traces the development of music up to the present day. Screens show images of past or contemporary stars, mixed with information about the milestones of each era. On video screens, music clips of Icelandic artists can be seen. Original costumes and instruments round off the collection.

Names like Elly Vilhjálms or Gunnar Jökull Hákonarson will be unfamiliar to most visitors from abroad, but they are more interested when the displays are devoted to musicians such as Emilíana Torrini, Sigur Rós, Of Monsters and Men and, of course, Björk. 'This list could be extended greatly,' says Tómas Young, the museum's managing director. 'That is the reason why a few musicians have complained that they have not been mentioned explicitly in the exhibition.' Rokksafn therefore puts an emphasis on interactivity. 'With a tablet, visitors can access additional information that we could not include because of a lack of space.'

In the sound laboratory, visitors are called on to demonstrate their own talent. Here drums, a guitar and a microphone are available for them to hold their own session. At the mixing desk they can mix a song the way they like to hear it.

For Tómas it is no surprise that Keflavík was chosen for the site of the museum. 'The roots of Icelandic pop and especially rock music are here.' In the 1950s, the American soldiers based in Keflavík brought new musical influences with them, and people listened to American radio channels. Thus the evolution of Icelandic rock music began in Keflavík, and the town was given its nickname: Rock City.

Rokksafn Íslands

THE ICELANDIC MUSEUM OF ROCK 'N' ROLL

Address Hjallavegur 2, 260 Reykjanesbær (Keflavík) | **Getting there** From Reykjavík take route 41 towards Keflavík, turn off right at Njarðvík and left onto Njarðarbraut; the museum is on the left after 2 kilometres | **Hours** Daily 11am–6pm | **Tip** On Njarðarbraut you can see the Stekkjarkot, a traditional Icelandic fisherman's house made from turf, wood and stone. Built between 1855 and 1857, it conveys a good impression of the way of life and manner of building of those days. The last residents left in 1924.

50__ The 66°North Shop
Clothes for adventurers on 'Fleece Street'

The four big Icelandic outdoor brands are crowded together in the city centre of Reykjavík within no more than 50 metres. On the upper part of Bankastræti, the shops of 66°North, Cintamani, Zo-on and Icewear stand opposite each other. That is why many locals jokingly call this spot 'Fleece Street'.

66°North was founded in 1926 by Hans Kristjansson and is the oldest of the four brands. Long before the invention of waterproof and breathable artificial fibres, Kristjansson learned in Norway how to make textiles that stood up to the wind and rain. His clothing was mainly produced for the fishermen and workers of Iceland, who were exposed, day in, day out, to rough climatic conditions around the Arctic Circle.

When Hans Kristjansson returned to his home at Súgandafjörður in the Westfjords, he founded Sjóklæðagerð Íslands – Iceland's factory for fishermen's apparel, known today under the name 66°North. Only two years later, Sjóklæðagerð Íslands kitted out the teams of the land and sea rescue service with jackets and trousers – the start of a tradition that has continued to this day. Before a new item of clothing goes into series production in the factories of 66°North in Latvia, the Icelandic emergency rescue teams try it out. 'For us there is no better way to test our products in real-life situations,' says Ólöf Helga Gunnarsdottir from 66°North. Today many walkers and fans of trekking tours are among the target group for the products.

The company runs 11 shops in Iceland to sell its weatherproof jackets, trousers and pullovers. One of them is on the above-mentioned Fleece Street, where competition seems to encourage brisk business and it is easy to compare prices. This street is probably the place on the island with the lowest probability of freezing to death – at least until closing time, and provided you have enough ready cash.

Address Bankastræti 5, 101 Reykjavík | Getting there Bus 1, 3, 6, 11, 12, 13 or 14 to MR | Hours Mon–Sat 9am–9pm, Sun 10am–9pm | Tip Cintamani, the shop next to 66°North, has a large pool in its basement. The big koi carp that swim here may not help customers to choose their clothes, but they keep an eye on things.

51 The Accident Memorial

More than scratched bodywork

According to a report by the World Health Organization, Iceland has one of the world's lowest rates of road traffic deaths. Nevertheless, accidents on the island often have a fatal outcome. The memorial on the Ring Road between Reykjavík and Hveragerði makes this clear in a most dramatic way. Beneath the wrecks of two crashed cars stands a sign with a cross and the question 'Eru beltin spennt?' (Have you fastened your seat belt?). The white number on the black cross shows the number of road deaths in the year so far.

The memorial was set up in July 2000 on the initiative of the Icelandic Traffic Council and the association of insurance companies. Placed on one of the country's busiest stretches of road, its purpose is to commemorate the victims of accidents and to remind drivers that the safety belt can be important in saving lives. In 2014, the island's drivers seem to have taken the warning seriously. In that year only three people died in traffic accidents, a historic figure lower than that recorded in any year since 1936.

Despite accident statistics that are relatively good, the roads of Iceland are a source of numerous hazards, especially for foreign visitors to the island. Fast roads of good quality can only be found in the region around Reykjavík. Most routes are two-lane, asphalted surfaces without a hard shoulder. Immediately behind the marker posts at the roadside there are often fields of sharp-edged lava that leave more than a scratch on the paintwork if you run off the road. Lack of experience with gravel and clay tracks, icy surfaces, single-lane bridges and sheep on the carriageway have been the undoing of many a driver. Potential for accidents that should not be underestimated also lies in the scenery of Iceland, which cries out for attention. Its beauty has often distracted drivers from concentrating on the traffic.

On the sign: 8 Látnir á árinu / Eru beltin spennt ?

Address Suðurlandsvegur, 110 Reykjavík | **Getting there** From Reykjavík via Ring Road 1 towards Hveragerði, then on the right 4.8 kilometres beyond the exit to Bláfjöll; the memorial is about 20 kilometres south-east of Reykjavík | **Tip** About 16 kilometres further east on the Ring Road you have a spectacular view of the plateau above Hveragerði from a car park.

52___Bæjarin's Beztu Stand

The celebrity sausage site

In appearance, Bæjarin's beztu stand is a small hot dog itself. The sausage seller stands in his narrow cabin, crammed in like a hot sausage in a roll, and hands out one hot dog after another through the hatch. Traditionally, this quick snack – Iceland's unofficial national food – consists of the inevitable frankfurter in a roll, lavishly covered with onions, ketchup and mustard. For inexperienced eaters of hot dogs this is an excellent opportunity to cover yourself liberally in sauce. Long-standing customers need only two or three bites to wolf down their snack. Often this happens while their second hot dog is being prepared. Thanks to these eating habits and the vendor's practised working pace, you never have to wait long until it is your turn, even though there is hardly a time of day when no queue forms at the stand.

The hot dog stall has been standing on exactly the same spot in Tryggvagata for decades – almost! Because of construction work on the neighbouring plot of land, in September 2015 it had to move from the place it had occupied for 72 years. Without much ado, a crane moved the little cabin four metres further away. A few months later it shifted a few metres once again, to make room for a new hotel. For the second time, customers coped effortlessly with the move, and of course the quality and products remained the same.

It all began in 1937, when hot dogs made from beef, pork and lamb were sold from a cart close to Lækjartorg Square. In 1940 the sales point moved to Kolasund, then in 1943 to its present-day location. Here it has satisfied the appetite of various international celebrities, including the American ex-president Bill Clinton, the Metallica singer James Hetfield, the former Guns N' Roses guitarist Slash and Joseph Simmons from Run-DMC ... and it is said that every one of them had to patiently take his place in the queue.

Address Tryggvagata 1, 101 Reykjavík | Getting there Bus 1, 3, 6, 11, 12, 13 or 14 to
Lækjartorg | Hours Sun–Thu 11am–1am, Fri & Sat 10am–4.30am | Tip If you don't
want to eat your hot dog standing up, walk a few metres across to Arnarhóll. In the little
park on the hill beyond Lækjargata are a few benches and a statue of the first settler in
Iceland, Ingólfur Arnarson.

53__Bar Ananas
Iceland's only beach bar

During the winter months, Bar Ananas (Pineapple Bar) in the centre of Reykjavík provides a feeling of summer for guests afflicted by darkness. Of course, the only beach bar in Iceland tempts them at brighter seasons of the year, too, with its fruity cocktails and Caribbean atmosphere. Bamboo hangings, palm-like plants and grass-covered parasols conjure up a tropical mood. Flamingos, parrots and other exotic creatures adorn the walls. And everywhere you look there are pineapples, for which the Icelandic word is 'ananas'.

An eye-catching feature of this newcomer to the nightlife scene of Reykjavík is the U-shaped bar counter on which gaily-coloured fish have been painted. 'The design is the work of the Icelandic artist Margeir Dire and the hip-hop musician 7Berg,' says Daníel Hlynur Michaelsson, the barkeeper. Behind the bar, old leather suitcases have been screwed to the wall. They serve as shelves for various alcoholic drinks that are just waiting to be mixed to make a delicious cocktail. 'In summer, fresh drinks, especially with gin, are in demand, but in winter it's cocktails with rumor whisky.' And Daníel Hlynur has also noticed differences between the sexes: 'The girls like strawberry daiquiris, the boys gin and tonic.'

The decoration comes to a climax in the basement, where a second bar is opened when the place is busy. Along the wall is a sinuous little strip of sand, which definitively turns Bar Ananas into a real beach bar. 'At first we wanted to cover the whole floor with sand, but that would probably not have been a good idea,' says Daníel Hlynur. 'We would never have been able to keep it clean.' When the DJs put on electro and dance beats at the weekend, it sometimes happens that a 'Flamingofant' gets spilled on the tiny dance floor – this is not a nickname for the bar's regular customers but a specially created house cocktail.

Address Klapparstígur 38, 101 Reykjavík | Getting there Bus 1, 3, 6, 11, 12, 13 or 14 to MR, then walk across Bankastræti and Laugavegur to Klapparstígur | Hours Mon – Sat 4pm – 1am, Sun 6pm – 1am | Tip 200 metres away at Laugavegur 36 is the Sandholt bakery, one of the oldest in Iceland. Now run by the fifth generation, it produces delicious bread, pastries and cakes.

54 __ The Barber's Shop

A haircut and shave on smuggled chairs

Wearing a beard has been trendy again for some years now – in Iceland as elsewhere. But of course! After all, whom could a beard suit better than a descendant of the Vikings? These days, however, it is recommended to take a little more trouble with facial grooming than the average Viking did around the year 900. The barber's shop Ragnars og Harðar is pleased to attend to this task – and has been doing so since 1957. 'We are the only barber's shop in Reykjavík that has existed for so long in the same place,' says Hörður Þórarinsson. Now a pensioner, he started his business in an era when a clean-shaven look was more popular than a well-trimmed beard.

The interior of the shop was modelled on a photograph of a barber's shop in the USA. 'The shaving chairs came from Denmark and were 10 years old even then – they were old smuggled goods,' he grins. They are not the only items with a history. Everywhere around the shop there are old-fashioned razors, knives and brushes that the founder used himself. 'In those days there was no such thing as a triple blade with flexible ball-bearings, and it wasn't easy to use a sharp cut-throat razor on your own face.' That is why the 400 workers from a neighbouring factory came to have a haircut and a shave. Now Hörður's son Ragnar Heiðar Harðarson runs the shop, where the fittings really are antique in comparison with those in other barber's shops, and are not simply designed to look old.

Many customers have grown old along with the shop, and still put their facial and head hair in the hands of Ragnars og Harðar. One of the regulars is the comedian and former mayor of Reykjavík, Jón Gnarr. Now and then a female customer turns up. 'If she wants, of course we cut her hair,' says Ragnar, 'and we ask her politely not to tell anyone else about it' – because this barber's shop is supposed to be an all-male preserve.

Address Vesturgata 48, 101 Reykjavík | Getting there Bus 14 to Mýrargata, then walk
across Bakkastígur to Vesturgata | Hours Mon–Fri 8.30am–6pm | Tip Above the barber's
shop stands the grey Landakotskirkja with a flat-topped tower that looks as if it has lost its
spire. It is worth walking through the residential area around this Catholic church to see
splendid houses, including the embassies of France, Russia and Canada.

55 _ Bike Barriers
Charmingly colourful obstacles

A bicycle is not necessarily the first choice as a means of transport in Iceland for going to a supermarket, a café or work. Perhaps that is why the authorities had a few old bikes to spare for the purpose of placing some colourful barriers on Laugavegur in the city centre. Since 2011 these barriers have ensured that this narrow shopping street is only accessible for pedestrians – and cyclists, of course – in the summer months (apart from restricted delivery times). The bike barriers have been placed, for example, at the corners of the street with Ingólfsstræti, Bergstaðastræti and Klapparstígur. On Vatnsstígur, too, a pink-painted bicycle forces drivers to turn off and guides them past Reykjavík's first hydrant, which represented the start of the municipal water supply on 16 June, 1909. Back then, fresh drinking water was conveyed through pipes into the city centre from cold springs and a river outside Reykjavík. The inhabitants then no longer had to rely on the poor-quality water from local wells. The result was an improvement in health and hygienic conditions, as well as in defence against fires.

The name of the street goes back to the women of Reykjavík, who used to walk along Laugavegur, which means the 'wash way', to reach the hot springs in the Laugardalur valley. Here they did their laundry. Today this busy street is populated above all by tourists, who come to buy new clothes – which they will later be able to wash.

Especially on the section of the street between the city centre and the Hlemmur bus station, clothes stores, some of them high-end, souvenir shops, restaurants, cafés and bars engage in lively competition for the masses of customers. After the shops close, Laugavegur gets ready for the party people: the street is not only known as a good place to go shopping, but also as a hotspot in Reykjavík's wild nightlife.

Address Laugavegur, 101 Reykjavík | **Getting there** Bus 1, 3, 6, 11, 12, 13 or 14 to MR, then walk to Vatnsstígur via Bankastræti and Laugavegur | **Tip** In the summer months, Laugavegur is crowded with tourists. If you would also like to see a few Icelanders, Saturday is a good day. When the weather is dry, the people of Reykjavík like to dress well and stroll through the city centre.

56__Bókin
Iceland's most chaotic bookshop

'It should be maintained in a permanent state of apparent chaos!' This statement, uttered by the British novelist John Fowles, is written on a faded sheet of paper that can be seen in the shop window of Bókin. As soon as you pass through the door, it becomes clear that the owners of this bookshop adhere strictly to Fowles' instructions: shelves of books, boxes of books, towering piles of books, tables covered with books. The whole place smells of old paper and bookworms. Eiríkur Ágúst Guðjonsson has the overview. 'The sorting of the books is randomly alphabetical' is his explanation of the system, and it takes a moment for the penny to drop.

In 1964 Bókin was set up as a second-hand bookshop. Today the stock consists of books of almost all ages. Ten years ago, Bókin moved to premises on Klapparstígur, which give the impression that a lot of books have been brought but few have been taken out over the years. 'Business is good, especially on our online shop,' says Eiríkur, and again you suspect that this man wearing a comic tie and a long ponytail is making a joke.

'Our customers come from all over the world, many of them from Russia or Germany. Above all, students who are looking for books about the Norse sagas come here.' He estimates the size of his stocks to be 40,000 or 50,000 second-hand books and maps. Most of them are in Icelandic, but if you have a little time to browse, you will find books in a wide range of other languages.

The late world-champion chess grandmaster Bobby Fischer appreciated the wide assortment. In the last years of his life, which he spent in Iceland, he passed many hours in Bókin. 'He sat at the end of a passage, wedged in between the shelves, and read all kinds of things,' Eiríkur recalls. 'If he didn't like a book, he tossed it away through the shop.' Which may well be the origin of the apparent chaos.

Address Klapparstígur 25–27, 101 Reykjavík | Getting there Bus 1, 3, 6, 11, 12, 13 or 14 to Lækjartorg, then walk along Hverfisgata to Klapparstígur | Hours Mon–Fri 11am–6pm, Sat noon–5pm | Tip 130 metres along Hverfisgata towards the harbour stands Iceland's blocky grey national theatre. It was opened in 1950 and has five auditoria of various sizes for 70 to 500 spectators. About 30 productions are performed annually.

57__C is for Cookie

Cake and coffee countered the crisis

'C is for Cookie', in contrast to the old-established cafés in the centre of Reykjavík, cannot point to a long tradition, but since it opened in 2010 it has built up a loyal customer base. The change of ownership in 2013 made no difference to this. 'Most things have remained as they were before,' says the new proprietor, Daniel Tryggvi Danielsson. 'I wanted to keep what the previous owners had established.' The furnishings consist of utilitarian wooden tables, a settee that is sagging somewhat, and lamps from grandmother's days. The low windows provide a good view of the little square in front of the café, the preferred place to sit when the weather is warm. It all makes a rather student-like impression, but it is cosy, and free Wi-Fi is part of the offer.

Before Daniel took over at C is for Cookie he had absolutely no experience whatsoever in the catering business. He was more often to be found in the pub scene than in the café scene – as a customer, though. As a result of the financial crisis, young men with a master's degree in international business were not in great demand at that time. 'I couldn't find a job, and when I walked into the café for the first time, I had the feeling it was right.' He quickly made his decision, since when he has been the master in the kitchen. 'As a child I often helped my mother with the baking, so I didn't find it difficult to learn the recipes for cookies and cake. From time to time I try out something new, but customers like the classics best of all.' That is easy to understand, as the oat biscuits and the cookies with dark chocolate and cranberries are unbelievably delicious.

He does his work at the oven so well that many guests did not even realise that the café had changed hands. 'That was the greatest compliment for me,' says Daniel with a smile – a café owner who does not drink coffee, but loves his own cookies.

Address Týsgata 8, 101 Reykjavík | **Getting there** Bus 1, 3, 6, 11, 12, 13 or 14 to MR, then walk along Bankastræti, Laugavegur and Skólavörðustígur to Týsgata | **Hours** Mon–Fri 7.30am–6pm, Sat 10am–5pm, Sun 11am–5pm | **Tip** 100 metres along from C is for Cookie is a record shop called 12 Tónar. Since 1998 a huge stock of CDs and vinyl records has been available on two floors. The music of many Icelandic artists can be found, as 12 Tónar has its own record label.

58__ The Christmas Trolls' Letterbox

One Santa Claus is not enough

Iceland has the lowest population density of any European country. Nevertheless, its inhabitants allow themselves the luxury of no fewer than 13 Christmas trolls instead of a single Santa Claus. And the trolls have their work cut out to handle all the wishes communicated to them in writing that are posted all year round in the red letterbox at Laugavegur 8. It stands directly in front of Litla Jólabúðin, where Christmas decorations are on sale the whole year round. For around 12 euros you can buy a letter there and write the address of a well-behaved child (or adult) on it. During Advent, this named recipient then gets a letter from the Christmas trolls. The red letterbox is emptied on 1 December. After this date the Christmas trolls have to work hard to answer all the letters because, according to Icelandic beliefs about Christmas, on 12 December they leave their cave in the highlands, one by one, and pay visits to people in the towns.

In the course of their long lives, the old trolls have acquired strange preferences that have given them their names. One of them is the foam thief Giljagaur, who likes to slurp the foam from freshly made milk. Another is the door-kicker Hurðaskellir, whose habit is to creep through the house and loudly slam open doors so as to give people a fright. The last of them to leave the cave, on 24 December, is the candle taker Kertasníkir, who steals the candles from the Christmas tree.

Despite these eccentricities, the Christmas trolls also bring along small gifts for children, which are placed in their shoes, laid out for the purpose, in exchange for cheese, milk or Christmas pastries. But take note: if you have been naughty, on the following morning all you will find in your shoes is an old potato.

POSTCARDS.
E CHRISTMAS SHOP.
ELL ISL.KR. 80.00
ISL. ISL.KR. 130.00

Icelandic

Santa mail box

This is not a regular mailbox

Letter s to the
Icelandic Santa

Write a letter with the name of
your best friend or your child and
get letters and gift from one of 13
Icelandic yule lads

This mailbox will be
emptied first December

e Little Christmas

Address Laugavegur 8, 101 Reykjavík | Getting there Bus 1, 3, 6, 11, 12, 13 or 14 to
MR, then walk across Bankastræti to Laugavegur | Hours Mon–Fri 10am–6pm, Sat
10am–5pm, Sun 10.30am–2pm (opening times of Litla Jólabúðin) | Tip If you don't
get to the letterbox on Laugavegur, you can post your message to the Christmas trolls at
the old harbour. By the ticket booths for the whale-watching boats on Ægisgarður you
can buy the letters to the trolls and use a second letterbox.

59 The Dead Gallery

Life with the death's head

Not death but a death's head dominates Jón Sæmundur Auðarson's Dead Gallery. It is situated a little bit out of the way in a back yard on Laugavegur, and the word 'Dead' adorns the wall next to the entrance. The paintings, T-shirts and caps, in fact almost everything in the small showroom, bear the symbol of death. Yet Nonni, as the lanky artist is usually known, does not think his art is gloomy. He sees even a death's head as a positive symbol. 'Everyone has a skull. That's something we have in common, and death is part of life.'

This was brought home to Nonni in 1994, when he was diagnosed as HIV positive. In the following years, of necessity, he thought intensely about the subject of death, and worked his fears into the 'Dead Concept'. The basis of this work is a Spanish proverb that Nonni made into his mantra: 'If you don't fear death, you can't enjoy life.' He has now printed this on countless T-shirts and translated the proverb into 16 languages. 'In 2004 more or less everybody in Reykjavík wanted to have one of these shirts. There was a real hype.'

Since 2005, Nonni's place of work has been his studio on Laugavegur. A few years later he also rented the gallery in which he sells his art. The two areas are separated by a bead curtain, beyond which lies an artistic chaos consisting of silk-screen printing equipment, cans of paint, countless brushes, canvases and all the other utensils that Nonni requires for his work. A narrow path leads through the middle of it all to his workplace at a computer. Here he develops his ideas, designs covers and writes songs. Nonni is the singer in the band Dead Skeletons, who were founded in 2008, originally only on the occasion of an art installation. They play a kind of psychedelic rock to accompany his vocals in a monotone voice. It's not light-hearted music, but that would not match the Dead Concept.

Address Laugavegur 29, 101 Reykjavík | Getting there Bus 1, 3, 6, 11, 12, 13 or 14 to MR, then walk via Bankastræti to Laugavegur | Hours Mon–Sat 1–6pm | Tip Right next to the entrance to the Dead Gallery on Laugavegur is the ironmonger Brynja. Since 1919 tools, screws and necessities for manual work have been sold here, which makes Brynja the oldest store of its kind in Iceland.

60___The Disaster Panels

The darkest hours in Icelandic maritime history

The visibility was only 1,500 metres when convoy QP-13, guided by the British naval ship *Niger*, sailed into a belt of mines north of the Westfjords on 5 July, 1942. In bad weather, the captain of the *Niger* mistook an iceberg for the coast. All five ships sank and 240 lives were lost in Iceland's worst-ever marine disaster.

The 18 mint-green panels that have been set up on concrete blocks between Harpa and Kolaportið record some 1,300 further accidents and losses at sea. The information was gathered from newspaper articles, archives and official documents. Mainly organised decade by decade, they show how dangerous the waters off the coasts of Iceland have been for ships and their crews. Pictograms, statistics and short texts show the viewer which ships sank or foundered, and where this happened. Then, as now, there were diverse reasons for the disasters: ships frequently collided with icebergs, caught fire, ran aground or got into trouble in unpredictable weather conditions. The years of the two world wars were especially perilous periods. The densely crowded symbols that cover the two and a half square metres of the information panels for the years in question illustrate this all too clearly. Sea mines, raids by U-boats and aircraft claimed the lives of hundreds of civilians and men doing naval service. In the early and the late 20th century there were also heavy losses of vessels from France, Norway and the Faroe Islands in times of intensive fishery activity.

In recent decades, navigation has become significantly less dangerous. Nevertheless, the choice of location for this open-air exhibition of the perils of going to sea might be thought insensitive, as it is right next to the quayside where the cruise ships anchor and put their passengers ashore. It is not the pleasantest greeting for holidaymakers starting an excursion on dry land.

Address Geirsgata (opposite Kolaportið), 101 Reykjavík | Getting there Bus 1, 3, 6, 11, 12, 13 or 14 to Harpa or Lækjartorg, then walk towards the quayside | Hours Open during summer months | Tip Next to the panels stands a locomotive, the *Minør*, dating from 1892. With its sister locomotive *Pioner* it was used in building the harbour from 1913 onwards.

61 _ The Einar Jónsson Museum

Modern art from the last century

Since 1923 the Einar Jónsson Museum has stood like a castle on the Skólavörðuholt hill. Next to the towering Hallgrímskirkja church, this building with a blocky appearance, which the people of Reykjavík simply call 'the museum', is only noticeable when you take a second look. When it was constructed, no other buildings of this kind existed. From 1920, even before it had been completed, it was a home and studio forIceland's most famous sculptor, Einar Jónsson, and his wife Anna. Today it holds the artist's legacy. His sculptures are characterised by Nordic gods, Icelandic tales and theological subjects. He always left the interpretation of his art to the beholder. Some 30 or 40 years ago, this attitude earned little recognition for Jónsson. 'Today it is young people, above all, who appreciate his work,' says Sigríður Melrós Ólafsdóttir, the museum director. 'His sculptures are full of symbols and tell stories.' The works appear modern, and do not in the least look as if most were made in the first half of the 20th century. With his artistic legacy Einar Jónsson has left to his homeland not only a valuable bequest, but also a burden. Before his death in 1954 he laid down strict rules in his will for the running of the museum. 'We are not allowed to change the exhibition, for example, or alter the museum building or admit too many visitors,' says Sigríður.

The idiosyncratic character of the artist, who is said to have had a taste for celebrating the occult mass, is not reflected in the conventionally bourgeois rooms above the museum in which he lived. On the other hand, the number of steps from the cellar up to his apartment, 52, is not a coincidence. The same applies to the seven symmetrically arranged rooms. These numbers stand for the weeks in the year and the days in the week, and exemplify Einar Jónsson's love of symbolism.

Address Eiríksgata 3, 101 Reykjavík | Getting there Bus 1, 3, 5, 6 or 14 to BSÍ, then walk via Smáragata and Njarðargata to Eiríksgata | Hours June–15 Sept Tue–Sun 10am–5pm, 16 Sept–Nov & Feb–May Sat & Sun 1–5pm | Tip Behind the museum is its sculpture garden, which was inaugurated on 8 June, 1984 and is open free of charge all year round. There, 26 bronzes give a good impression of the artist's work.

62 The Elf School
Fairy-tale time in Iceland

Belief in elves is widespread in Iceland and deeply rooted in the history of the country. It therefore comes as no surprise that there has been an elf school in Reykjavík for almost 30 years, though its 'pupils' might expect to find the classrooms in a mysterious and mystic place rather than in a crowded room in an apartment on an industrial estate.

Almost 10 in number, they are given an extremely warm-hearted greeting by the 'headmaster', and master storyteller, Magnus H. Skarphéðinsson – no wonder, as they are paying 43 euros each in 'school fees', not an elf-sized sum. In carpet slippers, track-suit trousers and a crumpled jacket, after a short round of introductions he starts the first lesson, devoted to elf theory. About half of all Icelanders believe in elves and 'hidden people'. They range from tiny to human-sized, and prefer to live in rocky places. 'So that people can't drive cars through their invisible houses,' says Magnus. Some of his pupils take the explanation seriously, others are amused.

The class consists of inquisitive tourists who believe in elves to a greater or lesser degree. Magnus dishes up entertaining stories to them in the following three or four hours, and pancakes with cream in the break. His tales are interrupted only when the participants report about their own experiences or Magnus passes round a 'genuine elf saucepan'.

It is said that even President Barack Obama had his attention drawn to the elf school. This happened when Obama met Magnus' brother Össur at a congress. Össur was foreign minister at the time, and was apparently checked by the US secret service. Obama is said to have asked Össur whether his brother Magnus really believed in elves.

'He definitely does,' replied Magnus with great conviction. And why not? After all, for three decades he has been giving lessons to pupils who share his belief.

Address Síðumúli 31 (2nd floor), 108 Reykjavík, www.theelfschool.com | **Getting there** Bus 2, 5, 15 or 17 to Laugardalshöll; take route 49 towards the city centre, after 4 kilometres turn right into Grensásvegur, at the second traffic lights left into Fellsmúli and then immediately right into Síðumúli | **Hours** Usually Friday 3pm, or by arrangement, see website | **Tip** About a 15-minute walk from the elf school is Laugardalur, a park and large recreation area that is also home to Reykjavík's zoo. It was opened in 1990 and, among other animals, there are foxes, reindeer and seals.

63 __ Elliðaárdalur

Reykjavík's green oasis

Unless a volcano is spewing sulphur oxide gases across the island, the Icelandic capital Reykjavík does not really have a problem with air pollution. A fresh breeze often blows across the city from the North Atlantic. All the same, it does no harm to have a 'green lung' like the Elliðaárdalur valley close by. This large park lies on the outskirts of Reykjavík, to the south-east of the centre, between two of the main roads into and out of the city, route 49 to Mosfellsbær and route 41 to Garðabær. When you are in the middle of this park, you will forget that you are in an urban district. Birdsong and the splashing sound of the river Elliðaár drown out the distant roar of traffic. Many narrow or broader paths wind through the woods, which is interspersed in many places by clearings with low vegetation. The park is a good place of recreation close to the city for walkers, and is also popular with joggers, cyclists, anglers and horse riders.

The valley was created about 4,500 years ago, when lava from a volcano on Bláfjöll flowed towards the sea and shaped this landscape. Today, apart from being a place for people to relax, it is a habitat for more than 25 bird species and some 320 kinds of plant. The dominant trees are birch, larch, Alaska willow, fir and pine. In addition to waterfowl – swans, greylag geese and mallard ducks – several species of wader birds, including oystercatchers and golden plovers, have found a home in the Elliðaárdalur. Both rabbits and mink have colonised the terrain.

The river Elliðaár is a rich source of nutrition for fish and waterfowl, thus making its contribution to this natural ecosystem. Every year, thousands of salmon swim upstream from the ocean to their breeding places, and many more fish hatch from the eggs that they lay. The Elliðaárdalur valley is full of activity – on land, in and on the water, and also in the air.

Address Rafstöðvarvegur, 110 Reykjavík | Getting there Bus 3, 11, 12, 17 or 57 to Elliðaárdalur; take route 49 towards the centre, turn right at the petrol station after 1.5 kilometres and left into Bíldshöfði, then left at the roundabout after 600 metres and straight ahead to Elliðaárdalur | Tip On the east side of Elliðaárdalur, an old power station stands on the river bank. Inside the transformer house you can see the old machines, which still produce 3,150 kilowatts of electricity in winter.

64_ The Expo Pavilion
The whole of Iceland in an underground car park

If you want to enjoy the glaciers, volcanoes and fjords, in other words to have the full Iceland experience, you need a lot of time, a liking for adventure, a generous travel budget and ideally a four-wheel-drive car. Visitors to the country who do not have these advantages, or only some of them, should consider taking a look at the underground car park at Harpa. Beneath this imposing concert and conference hall by the old harbour stands Iceland's expo pavilion from the world exhibition held in 2010 in Shanghai. Following its return from China, it represented Iceland at the Frankfurt Book Fair in 2011, and since then has found a permanent home down in the bowels of Harpa. The pavilion consists of a square room measuring approximately 30 square metres. Its walls and ceiling are covered with impressive film footage of the natural beauty of Iceland. The audience sit down or walk around while a volcano spews out its glowing red lava all around them. A few moments later, the atmosphere in the 360-degree cinema noticeably cools, and the viewers become passengers on a flight over a glacier lagoon with gigantic icebergs.

From Iceland's captivating natural world, the film switches in an instant to the capital city, which is equally beautiful. Among runners in the Reykjavík marathon, viewers get a close-up impression of the mood by the roadside and on the route.

Of course, these images are no substitute for the real experience, but the Icelandic production company, Sagafilm, has succeeded in making an atmospheric film that immerses its audience in fascinating corners of the country. In future, it will be updated regularly through the inclusion of the latest events, for example the eruption of Bárðarbunga in 2014. The 15-minute screening whets the appetite for real Icelandic adventures, so a visit to Harpa is a good way to spend a rainy afternoon.

Address Austurbakki 2, 101 Reykjavík | Getting there Bus 1, 3, 6, 11, 12 or 13 to Harpa |
Hours Mon–Fri 10am–6pm, Sat & Sun 11am–6pm | Tip Before seeing the expo pavilion,
don't fail to visit Harpa, which opened in 2011. Its striking honeycomb south façade was
designed by Ólafur Elíasson. Inside, the mirrored ceiling of the foyer is an eye-catcher.

65 Fljótt og Gott

Learn the art of dissection

With its long serving counter, sterile tables and a view of the waiting room, Fljótt og Gott by the BSÍ bus station is definitely not one of Reykjavík's top addresses, at least in terms of its atmosphere. However, alongside burgers and fries, this fast-food restaurant also has traditional Icelandic dishes on the menu. This means that a meal here is a good opportunity to try svið, boiled sheep's head, if you dare, in an anonymous environment. In contrast to a stylish restaurant, this snack bar is a place where it is easier to push a plate to the side almost untouched if you find your appetite has deserted you.

'Meet the meat,' says the waitress, placing half a sheep's head on the table. Its empty eye sockets, nose and protruding teeth immediately push the start button for a video in your mind's eye in which the living sheep is grazing in a green meadow. If you succeed in stopping the film, then first you have to remove the skin from the head in order to get at the meat beneath. Having completed your beginner's course in dissection, your palate is treated to meat that tastes little different from a normal piece of lamb.

Traditional svið is very easy to prepare. Before the half of a sheep's head is served, usually with turnips or mashed potatoes, the wool has to be singed off. Then the head is washed, split into two halves, and the brain is removed. After this, it is boiled in salt water until it is ready to eat.

Svið is a survival from an era when people could not afford to waste any part of the sheep at all. This is why the eyes are also eaten in some cases. At Þorrablót, especially, the Icelandic winter festival, svið features on the menu in combination with other traditional dishes. Icelanders like to wash it down with a glass of strong Brennivín spirit. If you have enough of this schnapps, sooner or later the film playing in your head might cease.

Address Vatnsmýrarvegur 10, 101 Reykjavík | Getting there Bus 1, 3, 5, 6 or 14 to BSÍ | Hours Daily 6am–11pm | Tip Above the BSÍ bus station stands a hospital, the Landspítali. It was built to designs by the architect Guðjóns Samúelsson between 1926 and 1930, and originally had only two departments. Icelandic women, who gained the right to vote in 1915, had campaigned for its construction.

66 Fótógrafí
Fishing with a camera

Like a lean-to made crooked by the wind, Ari Sigvaldason's little shop nestles between the other buildings on Skólavörðustígur in Reykjavík. The sign outside tells customers what to expect within: 'Fótógrafí' – images by Ari and three other Icelandic photographers.

In 2007 Ari, then a journalist, resigned from his job after 15 years and turned his hobby into his profession. He discovered his passion for photography at the age of 20, and although Iceland is brimming over with natural beauty that is worth capturing with a camera, he was more interested in people and towns. 'The mountain won't go away,' says Ari, 'but people are different. There is only one brief moment for getting a good photo of them.' He takes many of his pictures in Reykjavík or on trips across the country, and sells prints, most of them black-and-white, some in colour, in his green-painted shop.

'Fótógrafí is Iceland's first photo gallery of this kind,' says Ari. Setting it up was difficult owing to the financial crisis, but the business is now running well, which allows the photographer some freedom. 'Sometimes I simply shut the shop, put the number of my mobile phone on the door and set off to take new photos.' In doing this, Ari makes use of his not-so-new analogue cameras. When they are not in use, they hang in the shop as decoration, attracting many customers. 'Some people are more interested in the old cameras than in my pictures.' For music, too, Ari keeps faith at Fótógrafí with analogue technology: a record player provides the acoustic backdrop while customers browse through boxes of small and large-format photographic prints.

He regards himself more as a businessman than an artist. 'I don't have a plan and am not trying to convey a message when I take photographs,' he says, hanging a camera over his shoulder. 'I feel more like an angler with a lens.'

Address Skólavörðustígur, 101 Reykjavík | **Getting there** Bus 1, 3, 6, 11, 12, 13 or 14 to MR, than walk to Skólavörðustígur via Bankastræti and Laugavegur | **Hours** Daily noon–6pm, and on request | **Tip** Below Fótógrafí at number 4 is one of the oldest stone-built houses in Reykjavík. It was constructed from basalt in 1883 and now houses a Nordic Store with woollens, jewellery and sweets.

67__The Gods' Quarter
Life in the shadow of Odin

One of Reykjavík's residential quarters lies to the south-west of Skólavörðustígur, a busy shopping street. Most of the houses here were built in the early 20th century, when the gods of Nordic mythology were clearly favoured by urban planners. Several gods gave their names to the streets, and the district was therefore later given the name 'Asgard', home to the Æsir gods. However, this appellation is no longer used for the area.

When the street names were chosen, attention was paid to mythological relationships. Þórsgata and Lokastigur are close together, for example, just as the destinies of the gods Þór and Loki were closely connected. The situation is similar at the corner of Baldursgata and Nönnugata: the names refer to gods who formed a married couple – Balder and Nanna. Since 1998 Úlfar Eysteinssons has run the restaurant 3 Frakkar here. It is said to be one of the first that served sushi in Reykjavík, and includes whale meat and sea birds on its menu.

The architectural style of many of the buildings, with their large windows, is testimony to the days when they were small shops selling all kinds of goods. Until the mid-20th century these shops were an important social hub for the residents of the quarter. Then the little shops were put out of business by the arrival of large supermarkets. Only a few of them now remain, even though occasionally a new store, for example Kjöt & Fiskur, tries its luck in this residential area. At the corner of Berstaðastræti and Spítalastígur, Pavel Ermolinskij, an Icelandic professional basketball player, sells fish and meat with two friends.

In the early 20th century this kind of trading took place on Óðinstorg, the former marketplace. This is now the site of the design hotel Óðinsvé and its extremely popular and busy restaurant, called Snaps. There, many diners say, a god must be at work in the kitchen.

Address South-west of Skólavörðustígur, 101 Reykjavík | Getting there Bus 1, 3, 6, 11, 12, 13 or 14 to MR, then walk to Skólavörðustígur via Bankastræti and Laugavegur | Tip At the corner of Bragagata and Laufásvegur is Hlynur, a sycamore that is over 10 metres tall. The tree stands in the garden of an advertising agency and is said to be almost 100 years old. In winter it is covered with thousands of lights.

68__ The Handprjónasamband
Knitting for an income

'Icelandic wool has to be a bit scratchy. That shows that it is genuine.' Bryndís Eiríksdóttir knows what she is talking about, as she works for the Handprjónasamband Íslands – an association formed in 1977 for the marketing of hand-made woollens in Iceland.

Back then, about 1,000 women knitted pullovers, cardigans and hats in the winter months. In this way they improved their household income, as the woollens were sold in the shops in summer. 'But we encountered the same problem every year,' says Bryndís. 'The usual sizes and the most popular colours generally sold out quickly. And the rest often stayed on the shelf.'

In response to this, the Handprjónasamband Íslands took on the task of coordinating production. Since then, before the start of each winter, it has made a plan for who knits what, in which size and colour, and has sold the products in its own shop on Skólavörðustígur, and now also from a second outlet on Laugavegur. The shelves are piled high with thick woollens – most of them with the typical pattern of an Icelandic pullover, or 'lopapeysur'. 'We now also knit with thinner wool,' Bryndís explains. 'We have reacted to the wishes of customers, who want stylish clothes as well as warm ones. This has helped wool to become more fashionable again.' Today Handprjónasamband Íslands has approximately 400 members. How much they knit every year is something that varies widely, but everyone who would like to participate has to demonstrate his or her skill as a knitter. The association provides the wool for a test item. Bryndís does not conclude written agreements with the people who knit for the association. 'A handshake is enough. People know each other here in Iceland.' She also reveals that there is a man who regularly plies his knitting needles. 'I suspect that there are several men, but most of them don't like to mention it.'

Address Skólavörðustígur 19, 101 Reykjavík | Getting there Bus 1, 3, 6, 11, 12, 13 or 14 to MR, then walk to Skólavörðustígur via Bankastræti and Laugavegur | Hours Mon–Fri 9am–6pm, Sat 10am–4pm, Sun 11am–3pm | Tip A little further down the street is Iceland's oldest prison, Hegningarhúsið, recognisable by the surveillance cameras. Its usual name, 'the 9', derives from the address, Skólavörðustígur number 9. The prison contains 16 cells and was opened in 1874.

69__ The Héðinshús

Art on every corner

Reykjavík is a colourful city. Not only because of its red, blue and green roofs of corrugated iron and the outdoor jackets that the tourists wear when walking around, but also because some house owners appreciate a spot of artistic paintwork. In many places in the centre of Reykjavík, the streets are enlivened with art in the shape of large-format paintings and graphic work, small installations or elaborate graffiti. One outstanding example of this is the work of the Australian artist Guido van Helten on the Héðinshús. In 2014 he sprayed scenes from Jean-Paul Sartre's drama *No Exit* on its outer walls. He based these scenes on old photos of a theatre performance dating from 1961 in Reykjavík.

To go through the streets with your eyes open is to experience a visit to Reykjavík as a stroll around an open-air gallery. With free admission! 'A lot of people in Reykjavík like art, regardless of whether they see it in a museum or on the street,' says the street artist Sara Riel. 'Unfortunately, the city authorities did not share this point of view. In 2005, in a big clean-up campaign, many of the artworks, some of them illegal, were removed.' The street art scene did not allow itself to be influenced by this. Sara estimates that up to 100 artists are active on the streets of Reykjavík. Sometimes they get verbal permission from the owner of a wall or building before they set to work with a brush or spray can. But as a general rule approval has to be given by the city authorities, even in the case of private buildings, says Sara. 'But the prevalent mentality is to do it first, and ask afterwards.'

Few works are done to a commission; this is not the idea behind street art. 'We as artists want to participate in society and make our environment more interesting through our art, and give it meaning,' Sara comments. And that is more than colourful roofs and outdoor clothing.

Address Héðinshús, corner of Vesturgata and Ánanaust, 101 Reykjavík | Getting there
Bus 14 to Grandagarður, then walk towards the roundabout on Ánanaust | Tip The street-
art project Wall Poetry was part of the Iceland Airwaves 2015 music festival. Ten artists
took inspiration from musicians and bands to paint large-format murals. Some of them can
be seen on Laugavegur, Hverfisgata and Skúlagata, as well as at the Old Harbour.

70__The Hidden Burger Bar
Fast food from the broom cupboard

The snack bar Hamborgarabúllan at Bankastræti 5 cannot expect to get a lot of passing trade. The people who order a hamburger with fries here have not usually come in by chance. From outside, only the big shop window of 66°North and the bar B 5 are visible. It is possible to peer inside through the glass for a poor view of the dark interior, where definitely no snack bar is to be seen. During the day, not many customers take a seat at the tables in B 5, which is one of Reykjavík's fashionable locations in the evening. But if you venture inside, you will find yourself in a large room with a colourfully illuminated bar at the end. To the right of this, a passage leads to the toilets and the space behind the bar. And right there, in a room measuring only a few square metres, the Hamborgarabúllan burger joint has been in business since April 2010.

There are two poseur tables, a bin for waste and the kitchen equipment – the cramped space does not allow anything else. However, guests do not have to stay in this confined room, where surprisingly the air is not thick with the smell of fat, to eat their snack. They can take a seat in comfort at the tables in B 5. Hamborgarabúllan belongs to a small Icelandic chain of restaurants that was founded in 2004 by Tommi Tómasson, a trained chef with a qualification in hotel management. He is well known on the local culinary scene, having run a hamburger restaurant back in the 1980s, then later Hotel Borg for 11 years and then the Hard Rock Café in the Kringlan shopping centre for almost as long. Seven restaurants in Iceland now belong to Hamborgarabúllan, and the patties fried by this Icelandic company have also been well received in its snack bars in London, Berlin and Copenhagen. So to try one, you don't need to squeeze behind the bar in B 5. But when you are in Reykjavík, don't miss this hidden burger joint.

Address Bankastræti 5, 101 Reykjavík | **Getting there** Bus 1, 3, 6, 11, 12, 13 or 14 to MR | **Hours** Thu–Sat 11am–10pm, Sun–Wed 11am–9pm | **Tip** About 100 metres from B 5 in Ingólfsstræti is the toy shop Freddi. It stocks console games, fantasy figures and posters, as well as a good selection of classic video-game and pinball machines.

71__Höfði

The beginning of the end of the Cold War

When you say the name out loud, it sounds quite cute: Höfði. But there was nothing cute about the subjects that were negotiated in this white wooden house on 11 and 12 October, 1986 – nothing at all. At the so-called Reykjavík Summit, the US president, Ronald Reagan, and the secretary general of the Communist Party of the Soviet Union, Mikhail Gorbachev, met for talks about disarmament. Although this meeting between the two superpowers achieved no tangible results, it can be regarded as the beginning of the end of the Cold War between the western allies and the Soviet bloc.

In 1909, long before Höfði stepped into the glare of global publicity, it was delivered from Norway as a prefabricated construction kit and erected on the coast at Reykjavík for the French consul, Jean-Paul Brillouin. A low stone wall surrounds the premises, from where there is a sweeping view across the bay to the surrounding mountains. The design is a blend of various architectural styles from Art Nouveau and neo-Baroque to Norwegian National Romanticism. After Brillouin left, one of the occupants of Höfði (1914–1917) was Einar Benediktsson. A statue by Ásmundur Sveinsson commemorates this well-loved Icelandic poet. In 1938 the British consul and later ambassador moved into the white building. Visitors to it during World War II included the British prime minister Winston Churchill and the German actress Marlene Dietrich.

In 1958 the municipality of Reykjavík bought and renovated the house. In recent years it has been used for official receptions. In October 2015, 25 years after the reunification of Germany, the city acquired a piece of the Berlin Wall, a concrete slab weighing tons. This, too, symbolises the end of the Cold War and serves as a reminder of the summit meeting between Reagan and Gorbachev. The piece of wall has been set up in sight of Höfði.

Address Fjörutún, 105 Reykjavík | Getting there Bus 4, 12 or 16 to Hofðatorg; follow routes 49 and 41 towards the centre; after 5 kilometres on route 41, Höfði is on the left | Hours Viewable from the outside only | Tip On a bench next to Höfði is a QR code that you can scan with a smartphone, enabling you to hear a reading of a poem by Einar Benediktsson.

72 Hotel Borg
Where Marlene Dietrich slept

If you would like an overnight stay in Reykjavík in the atmosphere of the 1930s and 1940s, Pósthússtræti 11 is the right address. Here stands the elegant Hotel Borg in Art Deco style, with 99 rooms and suites. Parquet floors polished to a shine, high plaster ceilings with lamps in genuine period style, murals and spreading chandeliers bring back memories of the glory days after the hotel opened in 1930. It is no surprise that an icon of those days chose the Hotel Borg. 'The Hollywood star Marlene Dietrich stayed here,' says the concierge, Tómas Margrétarson. 'In the 1940s she entertained the American troops in Iceland.' Until the 1960s, the Borg was also the venue for popular dances with live music.

It was an Icelander, Jóhannes Jósefsson, who initiated construction of the hotel. A former wrestler who had competed in the Olympic Games in 1908, in the USA he became a member of the circus ensemble of 'The Greatest Show on Earth', and made a handsome fortune there. Following his return to Iceland, Jósefsson invested the money in the Hotel Borg. The building was planned by the state architect of the day, Guðjón Samúelsson, whose works, including Hallgrímskirkja and the National Theatre, put their stamp on the city of Reykjavík to this day. He had a similar success with the Hotel Borg.

The rather plain façade of the white concrete structure has deep-set windows and sparing decoration. Some of the rooms on the fourth floor beneath the mansard roof have a balcony. At a south corner Samúelsson included a kind of tower, which now accommodates the two-storey Tower Suite.

In the immediate vicinity, around Austurvöllur Park, stand the Dómkirkja and the Alþingishúsið. The latter, the parliament building completed in 1881, does not give the representatives of the Icelandic people any Art Deco atmosphere, but that would be too much to expect.

Address Pósthússtræti 11, 101 Reykjavík | Getting there Bus 1, 3, 6, 11, 12, 13 or 14 to Lækjartorg, then walk along Austurstræti to Pósthússtræti | Tip Not far from Hotel Borg at Austurstræti 16 is another building by the architect Guðjón Samúelsson. For almost 70 years it housed a pharmacy, and is now occupied by a restaurant and hotel, but the old name, Apotek (pharmacy), has been kept.

73__The Imagine Peace Tower
A light for world peace

'Imagine peace.' These words can be read in 24 languages on the white tiles of the Imagine Peace Tower on the island of Viðey off Reykjavík. The idea for the two-metre-high cylinder with a large platform made from various kinds of Icelandic stone derives from the artist Yoko Ono, the widow of the Beatle John Lennon.

Yoko Ono made this light installation in 2007 in memory of her murdered husband. Since then, the Imagine Peace Tower has sent a shining beam of light to heaven every year after dusk on the days from Lennon's birthday on 9 October to the anniversary of his death on 8 December. This bright symbol, combined with hope for more peace on earth, can be seen from far away. If you would like to experience close up the radiance of the Imagine Peace Tower, take the little ferry across to Viðey. The beam of the tower is also switched on between the winter solstice and New Year's Day, for Yoko Ono's birthday on 18 February and in the first week of spring. The power for the light is generated, as is usual in Iceland, from geothermal sources. This is said to have been one of the main reasons why Iceland was chosen as the site of this monument to peace.

The idea originated with Yoko Ono's 'Light House' art concept and was implemented in cooperation with the art museum in Reykjavík, the local energy providers and the city authorities. In 2008 the Icelandic postal service depicted the Imagine Peace Tower on a stamp, and even added the fluorescent face of John Lennon.

The message from the tower shines out far beyond Viðey, Reykjavík and Iceland. Via a wide range of social networks, by e-mail or postcards, people from all over the world can send peace greetings that are to be sent directly up to heaven with the light – perhaps with the intention that John Lennon will receive them there and pass them on with his urgent recommendation to a loving God.

Address Skarfagarðar (ferry terminal for Viðey), 104 Reykjavík | Getting there Bus 12 to
Dalbraut or 16 to Heðinsgata, then walk via Heðinsgata and Klettagarðar to Skarfagarðar;
routes 49 and 41 towards the city centre, turn right into Klettagarðar 1.7 kilometres
beyond the Kleppsspitali hospital, then left into Skarfagarðar | Hours Ferry timetable:
www.videy.com | Tip Right next to the Imagine Peace Tower is the Viðeyjarnaust hut.
It was built in 1986 and is a popular resting place for walkers in the summer. A charcoal
barbecue is available for everyone to use.

74__KEX Hostel

Iceland's hippest place to stay

In what was once a biscuit factory in the centre of Reykjavík, in April 2011 the KEX Hostel opened, and now offers its guests 142 beds in single or double rooms and dormitories. 'The large 16-bed rooms are almost always fully booked,' says Guðmundur Magnússon, a former teacher who manages the hostel, which is something like a cross between a factory, a gentlemen's club, an antique shop, grandmother's living room and a boxing gymnasium from the 1930s.

It was a matter of chance that new life was breathed into the old biscuit factory. In search of a movie location, the film director Óskar Þor Axelsson discovered the disused building in 2010. With five friends, including the footballer Eiður Guðjohnsen and the handball trainer Dagur Sigurðsson, he came up with ideas for Iceland's hippest place to stay overnight. The future 'hosteliers' drew up a list of phrases that they wanted to play a part in the design of the fittings and furnishings. The list included Neil Young, vinyl, beer, Björn Borg and beards.

Armed with these guidelines, Óskar's set designer Hálfdan Pedersen flew to the USA and Europe. He came back with huge quantities of unwanted church pews, lamps from World War II, cupboards from an old tobacconist's shop and leather for covering the seats. Great attention was paid to detail when the hostel was fitted out, so that falling asleep in one of the individually designed bunk beds is an experience. The walls of the common kitchens are covered with countless bingo tokens, and even the emergency exit routes have been decorated like classrooms.

The clientele of the KEX Hostel is international. In its restaurant, called Sæmundur í sparifötunum, travellers mix with locals from Reykjavík. Here you can enjoy a beer or a burger and listen to concerts by local bands before either going home or climbing a few flights of stairs to fall into bed.

Address Skúlagata 28, 101 Reykjavík | **Getting there** Bus 1, 3, 6, 11, 12 or 13 to Sæbraut/ Vitastígur or Sæbraut/Frakkastígur, then walk via Skúlagata | **Tip** At the back of the hostel is Hverfisgata. Number 12 on the corner accommodates two further parts of the KEX empire: Hverfisgata 12 – also furnished by Hálfdan Pedersen – mainly serves pizza and light meals. DILL, in the same building dating from 1910, is a more upmarket restaurant for Nordic cuisine.

75__ The Knife Maker
Cutting-edge artisan quality

The little hut in which Johann Vilhjalmsson sells his knives is hardly noticeable next to the bakery and the hairdresser's shop. It is a little way out of the city centre, close to Sundahöfn harbour. There is not much to look at in the confined interior except for a small showcase for the knives and a safe for the rifles that the gunsmith Johann repairs and sells. But anyone who is interested in hand-made knives will find Johann an expert partner for a chat. Since the early 1990s he has been making knives, and over the years his hobby became his profession. He learned the trade in Belgium, at L'école d'Armurerie in Liège.

'Although a lot of hunters in Iceland use a knife for their work, there was never a typical Icelandic knife distinguished by specific properties,' says Johann. So he simply produced his own design for an 'Icelandic hunting knife'. It consists of a blade of specially hardened steel, short at 10 centimetres, and a handle that is usually made from reindeer horn. 'This is extremely suitable for the job because it is light but very robust at the same time,' Johann explains. He makes his knives entirely by hand in his workshop, which lies a few streets away from the little shop. He sources the steel for his blades from Sweden.

They are heated for an hour in an oven at a temperature of 1,050 degrees Celsius, and then cooled. This produces the special hardness of the blades, which Johann then hones by hand. 'This is an art that not everyone masters.'

Depending on their taste, for the handle customers can choose between reindeer horn, walnut wood, whale tooth or buffalo horn. The price depends on the material, starting at about 350 euros and rising easily to a four-figure sum. Johann produces between 40 and 50 knives per year. Each one takes him about three days for grinding and polishing, and the meticulous assembly of blade and handle.

Address Dalbraut 1, 105 Reykjavík | **Getting there** Bus 12 to Dalbraut; Ring Road 1, then routes 49 and 41 towards the city centre, and turn left into Dalbraut | **Hours** Mon–Sat 2–6pm | **Tip** 500 metres from Johann Vilhjalmsson's knife shop is Laugardalslaug, Reykjavík's biggest thermal swimming pool. Next to it lies the national stadium, Laugardalsvöllur, with seating for 15,000, opened on 8 July, 1957.

76_ The Kolaportið
Iceland's tradition of flea markets

A place in which the customs department once stored confiscated goods is now the site of the Kolaportið flea market every weekend. On an area of some 2,400 square metres its visitors find a wide assortment of items. Practically everything that is to be found in Iceland's wardrobes, children's rooms and cellars is on sale in the old warehouse. From outside, only a few posters and the red-and-white Kolaportið sign reveal that there is a hive of sales and bargaining activity behind the brown wooden doors.

'Iceland's flea-market tradition is not long at all,' says Gunnar Hákonarson. He is the manager of Kolaportið and ensures that everything runs smoothly on its opening days. 'We held the market for the first time in 1989. In those days it took place on a car park in the open air' – with mixed results, as the island's changeable weather often deterred both sellers and purchasers. In 1994 the market moved to the old customs warehouse.

'On normal days we get between 8,000 and 10,000 visitors. If there is some special event going on in Reykjavík, the numbers are often higher.' Local residents, but also tourists, wander between the stands of second-hand clothes, home-knit Iceland pullovers, cheap Chinese goods, surplus and remaindered wares, curiosities and traditional Icelandic foods. If these things are to your taste, you can stock up on dried fish, fermented shark meat and beef tongue, or simply buy potatoes and vegetables. 'The grocery stands are usually at the market all year round,' says Gunnar – they have to be present because of the freezers. 'Otherwise we try to have as big a turnover as possible of different stands.' Families, boy scouts and sports clubs rent a stand in the hope of turning items they no longer need into ready cash. For both Icelanders and holidaymakers this is a guarantee of attractive bargains or original souvenirs from the island.

77__The Litla Kaffistofan
Coffee, petrol and football

Unless the petrol tank is running dry or the driver is dying for a cup of coffee, you might well speed past the Litla Kaffistofan, the little coffee shop. Possibly you will notice the green roof and yellow window frames of the white wooden building on Ring Road 1 between Reykjavík and Hveragerði, but you will not guess what awaits you behind the façade. Alongside hot coffee, cold drinks and a few snacks, the Litla Kaffistofan has an unbelievable array of football fan memorabilia – although they are not for sale. They are part of the remarkable interior of this service station, which was opened on 4 July, 1960 by Ólína Sigvaldadóttir. In 1993 Stefán Þormar Guðmundsson took over what is now Iceland's oldest snack bar on the Ring Road and began to adorn its walls with every imaginable item of football ephemera: team photos, fans' scarves, kit, club pennants and autograph cards. He had started his collection at the age of 10, and over the years had accumulated a considerable quantity of items. The customers liked it, so Stefán attached to the walls more and more of the fan mementos that he had brought back from his football trips or had been donated. Many European football clubs are represented in Litla Kaffistofan, from Manchester United to Borussia Dortmund. Among the more exotic memorabilia is an item from the Argentinian club CA River Plate.

In the Icelandic football league, soccer-mad Stefán hardly ever misses a game at ÍA Akranes, while in England his heart belongs to Tottenham Hotspur. But his all-time favourite club is Dynamo Kiev.

When asked what is the most valuable thing in his collection, Stefán has difficulty making a choice. 'That's like being asked which of your children is your favourite.' Finally, he decides to nominate an old photograph of two goalkeepers: Helgi Daníelsson for Iceland and the great Russian, Lev Yashin.

Address Suðurlandsvegur/Hvammsvegur exit, 110 Reykjavík | **Getting there** Via Ring Road 1, about 4 kilometres east of the exit to the 417 | **Hours** Mon–Fri 6.45am–6pm, Sat & Sun 7.45am–6pm | **Tip** About 10 kilometres east of Litla Kaffistofan is the Hellisheiði geothermal power station. Commissioned in 2006, it has a large exhibition on geothermal power and an earthquake simulator (daily 9am–5pm).

78__ The Men's Outfitter
British style for Icelandic gentlemen

In the basement of a branch of the discount supermarket Bónus on Laugavegur, a kind of secret treasure lies concealed. If you find your way through the plain-looking staircase, the moment you cross the threshold of the men's outfitter Kormákur & Skjöldur you will feel you have been transported to England in the twinkling of an eye. This is no coincidence, as much of the fittings come from a former clothes shop in London called Bertie Wooster. Warm lighting, deep carpets, wooden shelves of thick tweed jackets, royal red and dark green adorn the walls. In 2006 Kormákur Geirharðsson and Skjöldur Sigurjónsson heard that Bertie Wooster was up for sale. Although they were busy running their own bar at that time, they seized the opportunity, and only a week later suits, jackets and furnishings from the English shop were in a container bound for Iceland. Kormákur & Skjöldur opened for business with the goods brought from London, and the range was later extended with traditional British everyday clothing.

When checking the price tag on a tweed jacket or leather shoe, the interested purchaser might need a stiff upper lip, even though the store manager Guðbrandur Bragason espouses a different philosophy. 'High quality is important to us, so the prices are a bit higher. But our trousers, jackets and shirts will still be modern in a few years' time. British style is not subject to fashion trends.' In 2008, the shop was enlarged and a barber was installed. 'That livened things up, and my colleagues are now beautifully shaven and styled.'

Since 2010 Kormákur & Skjöldur has worked with the designer Guðmundur Jörundsson on its own small collections with classic lines. 'That is making us better known and attracting customers to our hidden shop,' says Guðbrandur. 'A lot of them like the experience of coming to us, being advised and perhaps buying themselves something fine.'

Address Laugavegur 59, 101 Reykjavík | **Getting there** Bus 1, 2, 3, 4, 5, 6, 11, 12, 13, 14, 15, 16, 17 or 18 to Hlemmur, then walk along Laugavegur | **Hours** Mon – Sat 11am – 6pm | **Tip** One block further along on Vitastígur is the boutique KRONKRON. It was founded by the designers Hugrún Árnadóttir and Magni Þorsteinsson, who are known for their colourful shoes. Alongside their own creations, the boutique sells dresses by exclusive designers.

79__The MicroBar
The centre of Icelandic beer culture

What's so micro about the MicroBar? The rooms in the basement of Restaurant Reykjavík are not small, nor are the prices or glasses. And the menu of drinks could easily be described as 'maxi'. The decisive factor in choosing a name is the contents of the glass, explains the barkeeper Steinn Stefánsson. 'We only serve beer from micro-breweries. In Iceland these include Kaldi, Ölvisholt, Stedji and ourselves, of course.' The owner of the MicroBar is the small Gæðingur Brewery from Sauðárkrókur.

The arrival of this bar in 2012 on Reykjavík's pub scene is the result of a small disagreement. Back then a pub in the city centre refused to serve beer brewed by Gæðingur, probably because a big brewery was insisting on exclusivity. The owners of Gæðingur reacted by opening the MicroBar. They brought Steinn, who used to be a poker player, back from the poker tables of New York to stand behind the bar counter in Reykjavík, since when his full house has no longer been a triple and a double set of cards but the refrigerated room behind his counter. This is where the barrels, but also some 200 bottles produced by small-scale breweries from all round the world, are kept. 'For some of these brews, we are the only place in Iceland where you can get it,' says Steinn.

This wide range of choice brings a lot of foreign customers to the MicroBar. 'A lot of them order our sampling tray, with small samples of the 10 or so Icelandic draught beers that we have on tap.' With this strategy, the MicroBar aims not only to help the nascent Icelandic beer scene to evolve, but also to change the drinking habits of many Icelanders. 'It is no longer necessarily the done thing to get blind drunk at the weekend. Gradually people are accepting the idea that you can drink two or three glasses for enjoyment during the week.' A good place to do this, with a broad selection, is definitely the MicroBar.

Address Vesturgata 2, 101 Reykjavík | Getting there Bus 1, 3, 6, 11, 12, 13 or
14 to Lækjartorg, then walk via Austurstræti towards Ingolfstorg | Hours Sun–Thu
4pm–12.30am, Fri & Sat 4pm–1.30am | Tip A few paces from the MicroBar in
Austurstræti is the boutique Gyllti Kötturinn, the 'Golden Cat', which sells new fashion
for women and out-of-the-ordinary vintage clothing. Even more extraordinary: the shop is
home to a cat that sleeps lazily in the window or watches customers trying on their dresses.

80 The Nordic House
A home for the Nordic peoples

Worldwide there are five Nordic Houses altogether, one of them in Reykjavík. Similar institutions, which are devoted to disseminating Nordic culture, are found in Finland, Åland, Greenland and on the Faroe Islands. The architect and designer of the house, which was opened in 1968, was Alvar Aalto from Finland. The white-painted single-storey building with its diagonally rising roof was one of his last works. The heart of this cultural centre is the library on the ground floor. Its holdings run to more than 30,000 items in the languages of the Nordic countries, including Denmark, Sweden, Finland, Norway, Greenland, the Faroe Islands and the Finnish region of Åland. 'We usually get the daily newspapers from these places a day after publication,' says the librarian, Margrét Ásgeirsdóttir. 'Our DVDs are also very popular, because Nordic films are not well represented on streaming platforms.' The users of the library are Icelanders who have lived in other Nordic lands or immigrants from those countries.

From the library with its high ceiling and large skylights, stairs lead down into the cellar. It is occupied by an art library containing 600 works by Nordic artists. Almost all of them can be borrowed, just like a book, to be displayed at home in a living room. The basement also accommodates changing exhibitions and a cosy little area where children can read. Concerts, readings and film evenings are held all year round in the Nordic House. For visitors who get hungry, there is the Aalto Bistro, run by the TV chef Sveinn Kjartansson. 'The restaurant is still largely fitted out with the original furnishings designed by Alvar Aalto, and serves both Nordic cuisine and a selection of the best from around the world.' The philosophy of the Nordic House can be seen in the same way: it aims to preserve its own culture but at the same time to be open for something new.

Address Sturlugata 5, 101 Reykjavík, www.nordichouse.is | Getting there Bus 1, 3, 6 or 14 to Háskóli Íslands, then walk along Hringbraut and Sæmundargata | Hours Library: Mon–Fri 11am–5pm, Sat & Sun noon–5pm; exhibition: daily noon–5pm; bistro: Sun–Wed 11am–5pm, Thu–Sat 11am–9pm | Tip Right next to the Nordic House is a bird reserve with a lake that the birds find attractive. From the raised seats here you can enjoy some bird-watching (beware of droppings!).

81 __ The Observation Platform

A magnificent view from a wonderful place

Looking north-west, in clear weather the view from the big observation platform reaches to the shimmering ice-cap of the Snæfellsjökull glacier. This is a distance of 100 kilometres, and towards every other point of the compass, too, you have a sweeping, almost unobstructed view. The viewing platform goes all the way round the glass dome of the Perlan hot-water reservoir and rests on one of its six aluminium tanks. To the north is the city centre of Reykjavík, with the imposing Hallgrímskirkja standing majestically above it. To the north-east of this is Reykjavík's local mountain, Esja, and the exit from the big harbour for cruise liners and container ships can be seen. If you walk clockwise round the platform, you can see that the neighbouring town of Kópavogur to the south merges with Reykjavík almost seamlessly. Through binoculars you can also make out Bessastaðir, the residence of the Icelandic president, to the south. With a little patience it is also possible to follow the air traffic to and from the inland airport to the west.

The decisive criterion when a location was sought in the 1930s for Reykjavík's first hot-water tanks was not the excellent view from the 61-metre-high Öskjuhlíð hill, but its elevated position. The pressure in the pipes that results from the altitude makes water supply in the city much easier. The old tanks have now been demolished and replaced by Perlan, which holds 20 million litres.

Despite the irresistible panorama, take time to look at the shining glass dome that gave its name to the hot-water tanks. During construction, an unbelievable 1,176 panes of glass were inserted into the metal frame, which is filled with warm water in winter and serves as heating for the restaurants inside. While guests enjoy their meal beneath the pleasantly warmed glass sky, the dome rotates 360 degrees every two hours.

Address Varmahlíð, 105 Reykjavík | Getting there Bus 18 to Perlan | Hours Daily
10am–9pm | Tip Inside Perlan an artificial geyser spurts water every few minutes. If you look
down to the foyer from the cafeteria, you will have a good view of the spouting jet of water.

82__ The Old Cemetery
A peaceful resting place

Death is a subject that the living prefer not to think about. When taking a walk around the Hólavallagarður cemetery, you will not necessarily be reconciled to the idea of death, but it is a consoling thought to note that there are such beautiful places for spending eternity.

Reykjavík's old cemetery lies to the west of the city centre. A low wall reduces the noise of traffic from the surrounding streets a little. Narrow paths, laid out in a right-angled grid, lead between the moss-covered graves. When the sun shines, light filters through the foliage of the numerous and varied trees, creating a magical atmosphere in this peaceful place. In 1838 the cemetery was inaugurated. The supposed honour of being the first to occupy a grave went to Guðrún Oddsdóttir. According to an Icelandic superstition, the first 'guest' in a cemetery becomes its guardian. This body does not decompose, it is said, and takes on the task of welcoming everyone else who is buried there. Guðrún's grave is adorned with an iron cross – the largest in the whole cemetery.

Originally Hólavallagarður was planned to accommodate 30 graves. As the years passed, it was extended 5 times, so that its present-day size is 3.5 hectares and more than 30,000 persons have been laid to rest there. In 1932 all the graves were occupied, and so a new cemetery was consecrated in Fossvogur. Nevertheless, it is now possible once again to be buried in Hólavallagarður.

'If you come to an agreement with the owner of the grave, you can place urns in older ones in which there is already a coffin,' says Heimir Björn Janusarson from the cemetery office. In recent years, this way of using the old burial ground has become more and more common.

'In 2015 there were more than 30 burials of this kind.' This brought back some life to the old cemetery, where the more attractive side of death is revealed.

Address Suðurgata, 101 Reykjavík | Getting there Bus 1, 3, 6 or 14 to Háskóli Íslands, then walk over Hringbraut to the roundabout | Hours May–Aug always open, Sept–Apr 7am–9pm | Tip A few famous people lie in Hólavallagarður cemetery, including Hannes Hafstein, the first prime minister of Iceland, and the painter Jóhannes Sveinsson Kjarval, who died in 1972. A large, six-sided column of basalt adorns his grave (plot E 8-51).

83___Öskjuhlíð
The hill of wild rabbits

What do Icelanders do when they lose their way in the woods? They stand up! This joke refers to the scarcity of tall trees in Iceland. A good place to find out whether this still holds true is in Reykjavík's largest forest, Öskjuhlíð. More than 170,000 trees have been planted since the 1950s on the hill, which rises to a height of 60 metres near the city centre. With the shining dome of the Perlan hot-water reservoir (see ch. 81) at the summit, it is a conspicuous landmark of the Icelandic capital.

In this recent woodland of birch, fir and pine, sparrows, thrushes and many other kinds of bird feel at home. But Öskjuhlíð has also been adopted by a large number of rabbits. This colony was not founded voluntarily, however, as most of them are the descendants of domestic rabbits that were taken to the hill and left there. With a little luck, walkers and cyclists on the winding paths around the hill will encounter these semi-wild bunnies, which are always on the lookout for something good to eat.

For the citizens of Reykjavík, Öskjuhlíð is above all a place to go walking or to ride a bike. In World War II it was a military base for British and American forces. The remains of a few bunkers and old barracks around the hill still bear witness to this. In the early 19th century, Öskjuhlíð was used as a quarry. For construction of the harbour from 1913 onwards, great quantities of its basalt rock were required. Two steam locomotives hauled wagons with heavy loads of stone towards the sea on specially laid railway tracks.

Of course, the history of Öskjuhlíð goes back much further than this. The hill originated in a volcanic eruption during the last ice age, and was covered by a glacier approximately 10,000 years ago. At that time, the sea level was considerably higher than it is today, and more than half of the hill then lay beneath the surface of the sea.

Address Varmahlíð, 105 Reykjavík | Getting there Bus 18 to Perlan or 5 to Nauthólsvík – HR | Tip At the tip of Öskjuhlíð, right next to the Perlan water tanks, stands the sculpture *Dansleikur* by the deceased artist Þorbjörg Pálsdóttir. It depicts four people dancing. Not far away is a small, artificially created geyser.

84 Phallic Donations

Exhibitionists, posthumously

In 2011, the Icelander Páll Arason died at the age of 95. He is said to have had a few acquaintances among the ladies, but he became truly famous in the country because after his death he donated his pride and joy. It is on display in the Phallus Museum in Reykjavík, which now not only possesses the phalluses and penile parts of all Icelandic animal species but also has a specimen deriving from Homo sapiens. More of them will be collected, if the curator Hjörtur Gísli Sigurðsson has his way. 'We have a few declarations of intent, but before this takes effect, the men have to get approval from various public authorities.' The American Tom Mitchell has already been through this procedure. A donor certificate for his penis, which he calls 'Elmo' and has made costumes for, is already hanging in the museum.

In the museum premises on Laugavegur you can find more penises than at happy hour in a strip club. Hjörtur's exhibition contains over 300 examples of the male sexual organ, in practically every size: from the metre-long appendage of a blue whale, preserved in formalin, to the tiny penis of a domestic mouse displayed close by.

The starting point for the Phallus Museum as it is today was a dried bull's penis, which was given as a joke to Hjörtur's father, Sigurður Hjartarson, by friends in 1974. In the following years, the collection swelled to an imposing size. 'Before too long, people would phone my father and ask if he wanted to have the penis of a beached whale or some other animal,' Hjörtur recalls. Finally, in 1997 Sigurður opened a museum with 60 exhibits in Reykjavík, and since then the collection has grown continuously. In 2015 about 30,000 visitors came to the Phallus Museum, among them tourists, stag parties and school groups. 'More women than men come to the museum. The men often wait outside,' says Hjörtur. Perhaps they want to avoid comparisons.

Address Laugavegur 116, 105 Reykjavík | Getting there Bus 1, 2, 3, 4, 5, 6, 11, 12, 13, 14, 15, 16, 17 or 18 to Hlemmur | Hours Daily 10am–6pm | Tip On the next corner in Rauðarárstígur is Iceland's biggest record shop, Lucky Records. In its stocks are 40,000 vinyl records and CDs for all styles of music. The shop has a small stage on which local bands sometimes perform.

85 Police Headquarters

Police work in novels and social networks

The sometimes gloomy and rather anti-social detective Inspector Erlendur Sveinsson is one of the finest among the Reykjavík police force. His place of work at Hverfisgata 113–115 is very well known to millions of readers of the novels of the Icelandic crime writer Arnaldur Indriðason. And in real life, too, crimes are solved here, as this building opposite the Hlemmur bus station is the headquarters of the 'genuine' police.

'The building dates from some time in the 1960s,' says Þórir Ingvarsson. At Lögreglan, as the police force is called in Iceland, he is responsible for publicity work, among other tasks. The old-fashioned brown wooden doors, the grey linoleum floor and the rickety lift confirm his assessment. The five-storey building with mirror glass in some of its windows exudes the shabby charm of bygone days. The newly renovated extension does little to change this impression.

In contrast to its premises, Lögreglan is bang up to date on the subject of social media. Since 2010 it has been represented in networks like Facebook, Twitter and YouTube. Þórir also looks after an Instagram account that is one of the most popular in all of Iceland. This portal for images is used not only to publish photos of break-ins, finds of drugs and traffic controls. 'Often my colleagues post snapshots of their midday break or bits of fun during work.' In this way the police force, which consists of only 660 police officers in the whole country, aims to stay in close contact with citizens. The officers also adhere to this strategy by going out on the beat unarmed. 'Without a weapon you get closer to people than with one.' Although Reykjavík may seem like a peaceful place, he adds, of course there is drug dealing, organised crime, smuggling, and the occasional murder. Plenty of work for Inspector Erlendur and for his real-life colleagues at Lögreglan.

Address Hverfisgata 113–115, 105 Reykjavík | **Getting there** Bus 1, 2, 3, 4, 5, 6, 11, 12, 13, 14, 15, 16, 17 or 18 to Hlemmur | **Hours** Viewable from the outside only | **Tip** The public square opposite the police headquarters is Hlemmur – a hub for many bus routes since 1970. In summer 2017, Hlemmur Mathöll opened in the bus terminal there. It means Hlemmur Food Hall, and has cafés, bars and restaurants.

86 Reykjavík Chips
Spanish fries, made the Belgian way

Small, large or family size – and 10 different sauces to put on them. The menu is not extensive in what is probably the first snack bar in Iceland that makes French fries in the Belgian manner. Shiny green tiles and wood dominate the interior of this little eatery with its modest seating. The fries are served in cardboard cones, and holes have been bored in the tables to keep these in place.

The founders of this relatively new fast-food joint are local celebrities, including the successful musician Ólafur Arnalds, the R&B singer Friðrik Dór Jónsson and the actor Arnar Dan Kristjánsson. The last-named got to know the advantages of chunky-cut fries in Milan, not at some motorway service station in Belgium. On his return from an engagement in northern Italy, he brought the idea for the snack bar with him. 'I wanted to offer something fresh and new in Iceland,' says Arnar Dan. So he asked the Italians to give him the recipe and some tips on the best way to fry the potatoes. There followed five months of hard work – for the brain and the stomach – before the opening took place on Iceland's national day on 17 June, 2014. The company logo with chips in the shape of the Hallgrímskirkja and the fittings had to be designed, and the right kind of potatoes for the fries had to be found. 'I lived on practically nothing but potato chips for four months,' recalls Arnar Dan, the person mainly responsible for the project. 'We get the potatoes from Spain, boil them, and then deep-fry them twice.'

The celebrity owners are not to be found frying potatoes in person. 'Ólafur has no time at all for that, because he spends a lot of time on tour,' says Arnar Dan, who wants to continue as an actor and not only pursue his career as a snack-bar king. Nevertheless, it is worth calling in at Reykjavík Chips, because the taste matters much more than the cook.

Address Vitastígur 10, 101 Reykjavík | Getting there Bus 1, 2, 3, 4, 5, 6, 11, 12, 13, 14, 15, 16, 17 or 18 to Hlemmur, then walk along Laugavegur to Vitastígur | Hours Mon–Fri 11.30am–10pm, Sat & Sun 11.30am–11pm | Tip Directly opposite Reykjavík Chips is the music shop Geisladiskabúð Valda, where second-hand and new vinyl records, CDs, DVDs and video games have been sold since 1998.

87 __ Reykjavík International Airport

Where flying is like catching a bus

Get to the terminal 30 minutes before take-off, buy a ticket and wait for the boarding announcement. At Reykjavík's small international airport, flying is almost like catching a bus. Not far from Lake Tjörnin in the urban area, three runways, all short at between 960 and 1,567 metres, cross the Vatnsmýri marshland. In comparison to its big brother at Keflavík, the airport gives the impression that everything has shrunk. The walk from the ticket counter to the waiting zone takes as much as 15 seconds if you have a heavy suitcase, and half as long if you only have hand luggage. The size of the sole baggage conveyor is also modest, and when passengers board, the aircraft taxis right up to the ground-floor gate.

After take-off, you hardly have time to drink a cup of coffee before the propeller plane is already preparing to land again. The flight destinations in Iceland include Akureyri, Egilsstaðir, Ísafjörður and a number of other small domestic airstrips. There are also connections to Greenland and Vestmannaeyjar (the Westmann Islands).

The first plane to take off from Reykjavík International Airport was on 3 September, 1919. This was the beginning of aviation in Iceland, but it was not until 1938 that regular flights took off from Reykjavík. Before British forces took control of the airport in 1940, its runway was a strip of grass. Later, the marshy land was made firm with huge quantities of gravel, and the runways acquired a surface of tar. Because it is immediately adjacent to the Landsspítali, Iceland's biggest hospital, the airport has a major role in rescue flights. Despite this, plans have been presented to move it outside the city. Land for building is scarce in Reykjavík, and in future housing could be built on the site where 367,000 passengers landed and took off in 2014.

Address Þorragata 10, 101 Reykjavík, www.isavia.is/flugvellir/reykjavikurflugvollur |
Getting there Bus 15 to Þorragata | **Hours** At flight times | **Tip** To the north of the
airport lies the campus of the University of Iceland. The main building, then one of the
most splendid in the country, opened on 17 June, 1940. In front of it stands Ásmundur
Sveinsson's sculpture *Sæmundur á selnum*.

88 Reykjavík Roasters
Perfect coffee comes from weighing and sniffing

Whether you drink coffee for pure pleasure, as a stimulant or simply as a social activity, you should not miss out on a visit to Reykjavík Roasters. In this inconspicuous café on the little square between Kárastígur and Njálsgata, they know how to entice extremely fine aromas from a coffee bean. This is not done by using artificial flavour enhancers but by the way they roast the beans and make the coffee.

'The right quantities of water and ground coffee are the decisive thing. That is why we grind the beans freshly and weigh out the ground coffee very precisely before it goes in the machine,' says Ingibjörg Sigurðardóttir, a co-founder of Reykjavík Roasters. This principle makes the process labour-intensive, but they adhere to it strictly, no matter how many people are queuing at the counter.

Ingibjörg acquired her knowledge of coffee over several years. She attended seminars in Europe and did training in West Africa. In 2008 she founded Kaffismiðja Íslands, the predecessor of Reykjavík Roasters, which has been in business since 2013. She and her colleagues developed their own method of roasting coffee beans. They are sourced directly from farmers in Columbia and from local or Norwegian importers. 'We only give the beans a light or medium roasting. In that way, we avoid the presence of the bitter elements that you can taste in a lot of the coffee that comes from supermarkets.' The beans stay in the machine for 30 to 40 minutes, and the right moment to take them out is decided according to the aroma. The tasting happens later – with both hot and cold coffee. 'The lightly roasted beans develop sweeter aromas that taste of chocolate or caramel,' says Ingibjörg.

The people of Iceland are crazy about coffee, and Reykjavík Roasters seem to have hit the right note. The cosy café with its blue roasting machine is usually full of customers.

Address Kárastígur 1, 101 Reykjavík | Getting there Bus 1, 2, 3, 4, 5, 6, 11, 12, 13, 14, 15, 16, 17 or 18 to Hlemmur, then on foot via Laugavegur and Frakkastígur to Kárastígur | Hours Mon–Fri 8am–6pm, Sat & Sun 9am–6pm | Tip About 70 metres above the café is a small park where benches are an inviting place to linger and drink a takeaway coffee.

89___Reykjavík Soundwalk
Sounds of the city

Put on your headphones, switch on your MP3 player, and off you go on the Reykjavík Soundwalk. This is a circuit through the city, a little off the beaten tourist track, that takes in places of interest such as the Hallgrímskirkja, the Harpa concert hall and the Tjörnin lake. 'Soundwalkers' hear through their headset the sounds of piano, percussion, electronic samples and voices, combined with the acoustic background of the streets. Visitors to the city can download the MP3 file for free from the Soundwalk internet site.

Students at the art school produced this acoustic guided walk in a seminar entitled 'Sound of Nature – Sound of the City'. The intention of this collage lasting almost one hour is to enhance perception of the urban environment, making the street scene audible.

'The course participants took inspiration from the shapes of buildings and imagined how the architecture would send back a sound,' explains their teacher, Marie Guilleray. 'Then they incorporated this into their composition.' Marie, who is French, is a sound artist herself and has created soundwalks. The Reykjavík Soundwalk is an individual experience, she says, because everyone perceives the world around them in a different way. Correspondingly, the students' compositions proved to be full of variety.

The work went on for two years until the sound collage and the website, including a facility for downloading, were completed in 2015. Taking part in the Reykjavík Soundwalk is not a guided tour in the classic sense but an experience that anyone can have in the city at any time. It is also suitable for children from the age of eight. 'For younger ones, the sounds might seem a little bit scary,' says Marie Guilleray.

Soundwalkers should ideally use headphones that do not completely cut out all noises from the surroundings. 'That way, you can hear the sounds of the city live.'

Address Eiríksgata (start at Hallgrímskirkja), 101 Reykjavík, www.soundwalkreykjavik. wordpress.com/portfolio/download | Getting there Bus 1, 3, 5, 6 or 14 to BSÍ, then walk to Eiríksgata via Smáragata and Njarðargata | Tip At the lake, it is worth interrupting the soundwalk briefly. The old Hljómskálagarður Park has attractive flower beds, an avenue of birches and a number of sculptures. Next to the bridge is the old Hljómskálinn music school, Iceland's 'first' concert hall.

90__ The Sculpture and Coast Path

An open-air exhibition with a view

Reykjavík's Sculpture and Coastal Path leads eastwards along the water from Harpa to the Laugarnes headland. Apart from the artistic architectural form of the concert hall, the first sculpture is *Sólfar*, the 'sun traveller', by Jón Gunnar Árnason. This stainless-steel model of a Viking ship was unveiled in 1990, a year after the death of the artist. About 250 metres further on, Johann Eyfells' work *Íslandsvarðan* stands; this weathered sculpture looks like a big chunk of lava. The next work of art, somewhat inconspicuous, is *Fjöruverk* by the conceptual artist Sigurður Guðmundsson. It consists of several large stones in the coastal embankment. They are colourful, shiny and polished smooth. It is easy to stroll past without noticing them, especially when the view of Faxaflói Bay distracts you.

When you reach the Höfði you will encounter the sculpture *Partnership* by Pétur Bjarnason. It consists of two half-arrows of bronze pointing to the heavens, and was donated by the ambassador of the US on 4 July, 1991 on the occasion of the 50th anniversary of the beginning of diplomatic relations between Iceland and the USA. An identical sculpture has been erected in Miami. It also symbolises the connection between the two countries through the Gulf Stream, which flows from the Florida coast up to Iceland.

Shortly before Sæbraut makes a sharp turn to the right, the Sculpture and Coastal Path heads off left to Laugarnes. The private house of the Icelandic film director Hrafn Gunnlaugsson, maker of Viking movies, stands here. From the road, his wild art made from recycled materials can be seen in a garden that is equally wild. Only a few metres further on, the museum of the deceased sculptor Sigurjón Ólafsson brings this art trail to a conclusion.

PARTNERSHIP

Address Sæbraut, 101 Reykjavík | Getting there Bus 1, 3, 6, 11, 12 or 13 to Harpa | Tip
By the Sigurjón Ólafsson Museum, a walking trail leads onto the Laugarnes headland past
several historic sites such as an old church and a hospital in which lepers were treated from
the late 19th century. It burned down in 1943.

91 The Shipyard
The place to come when rust shows through

Wedged into the huge steel framework on the slipway of the shipyard, boats in the Old Harbour of Reykjavík can be seen out of the water. Their great bulks loom immediately next to restaurants, shops and a hotel. Only a low fence separates the shipyard from the other parts of the harbour, and the smell of paint often hangs in the air when a vessel's hull needs some cosmetic improvement.

The dock was built in Scotland in 1902, transported to Reykjavík and enlarged a few years later to take bigger ships. 'It only takes an hour or so to raise a fishing trawler that needs repair out of the water and on to the dock,' says Bjarni Thoroddsen, an employee of Stálsmiðjan-Framtak, the company that operates the shipyard. This task is carried out using heavy steel chains that have to be replaced every 10 or 12 years as they are subjected to severe wear and tear. Two slipways to handle ships with a length of up to 85 metres and a weight of up to 2,400 tonnes are at the company's disposal. The vessels repaired here are mostly fishing boats, approximately 40 of them every year. On a visit to Reykjavík you therefore have a good chance of seeing a ship out of the water for repairs.

Since 1933, Stálsmiðjan-Framtak has taken care of all matters required by ship owners. This includes overhauling the engines, welding work on their hulls, removing rust, painting, replacing and repairing fishing equipment, and seeing to the steering and power mechanisms. Until 35 years ago, ships were still built in the Old Harbour, but stiff competition from Spain, Turkey and Chile has made this business unprofitable. Stálsmiðjan-Framtak built a total of 36 trawlers with a length of up to 68 metres. In 1955, the first boat made of steel that was ever built in Iceland was launched from this shipyard – a 1,000-horsepower tug for the Reykjavík port authority.

Address Ægisgarður, 101 Reykjavík | Getting there Bus 14 to Mýrargata, then on foot via Mýrargata to Ægisgarður | Hours Viewable from the outside only | Tip On Mýrargata, about 250 metres further out from the centre, is a small children's playground with an old fishing boat. The playground equipment has been made from rope, wooden beams and fishing nets.

92___The Smekkleysa Record Shop

The name is misleading

The range of items found in the Smekkleysa record shop is far from being in bad taste, even though that is what the name means. Behind the green façade of this small store you will find a wide selection of music by Icelandic artists on vinyl and CD. This well-stocked music shop is also an important element in the story of Icelandic music, as it is associated with the Smekkleysa label. In 1986 it was established by a collective of artists from which the well-known band The Sugarcubes later emerged. 'The first publication under this label was not a CD but a postcard whose theme was the Russian-American disarmament summit in Reykjavík between Ronald Reagan and Mikhail Gorbachev,' recalls Ásmundur Jónsson, one of the founders of the label. 'The first single by The Sugarcubes was produced with the proceeds from selling the postcard.' The band's singer at that time was Björk Guðmundsdóttir, who later enjoyed – and today still enjoys – great success worldwide as a charismatic solo artist. The Sugarcubes were the leading act recording on the label until they split up in 1992. After this, Smekkleysa took a break to recharge its creative batteries and did not resume work until 1994. Björk has kept faith with the label to this day as far as her releases in Iceland are concerned. The same applies to internationally known bands such as GusGus, Sigur Rós or Dikta. 'For new bands, above all, it is important to have an Icelandic label, because we maintain contacts to the market here,' says Ásmundur. And artists who succeed in Iceland also attract attention in Europe and America.

The shop in the city centre has existed since 2001. Here the Smekkleysa label sells the music of its own bands and also that of other artists. If you are looking for the latest inside information about the Icelandic music scene, here you are definitely in the right place.

Address Laugavegur 35, 101 Reykjavík | **Getting there** Bus 1, 3, 6, 11, 12, 13 or 14 to MR, then walk via Bankastræti and Laugavegur | **Hours** Mon – Fri 10am – 6pm, Sat 10am – 5pm, Sun noon – 5pm | **Tip** After all this music history, some refreshment is called for. About 300 metres away at Bergstaðastræti 1 is the bar Kaffibarinn where the British singer Damon Albarn, the front man of Blur, has often been seen. For years it has been rumoured that he is joint owner of the bar.

93 Stella Boutique

When you get cold feet

For Icelandic women, there really are a lot of occasions in the course of a year to get cold feet or even cold legs. Even in the summer months, a fresh wind frequently blows across the country, and those who insist on wearing a fashionable skirt make sure they put on tights. At the Stella boutique the demand for a range of products was recognised long ago, which is why Edda Hauksdóttir has a wide choice of unusual and also conventional tights in her assortment.

The family has been running this shop in Bankastræti ever since 1942. Originally her father had a factory outlet for dresses there. Later, cosmetic items were added to the range of goods, and at some stage they started to stock tights as well. 'When I was only seven years old I used to help my father in the office after coming home from school. For me there was never any question of choosing a different career,' Edda recalls.

In decorating the shop window she opts for eye-catching tights. Comics, the heads of cats, flowers and net patterns adorn the plastic legs of the dummies. 'A striking pair of tights changes your whole appearance. In this way, you can make an expensive outfit look completely different, even with low-cost tights,' Edda explains. Customers gain the benefit of all her experience. 'I only need to estimate their height, and I know straight away which pair of tights will fit.' That is why it is no problem for Edda to sell tights to a husband buying for his wife. 'As long as he knows how tall she is.'

Before tights were sold in the building with the Stella sign – it was built from basalt stone in 1881 – a print works and the state bank, the Landsbanki, founded in 1886, were housed there. The name of the street, Bankastræti, goes back to those days. In contrast to Stella, the bank only stayed here for a few years. So it's time for a new name: 'Tights Street'.

Address Bankastræti 3, 101 Reykjavík | **Getting there** Bus 1, 3, 6, 11, 12, 13 or 14 to MR, then walk to Bankastræti | **Hours** Mon–Sat 10am–6pm, Sun 1–5pm | **Tip** Stella's immediate neighbour is the prime minister, whose office is in the Stjórnarráðshúsið, on the lawn next to the stocking shop. Two statues stand in front of this former prison: on the right Iceland's first prime minister, Hannes Hafstein, and on the left King Christian IX of Denmark.

94_ The Viðey House
The home of powerful men

From the Skarfabakki ferry terminal, the trip across the bay to the island of Viðey off Reykjavík takes less than five minutes. During the crossing the white Viðey House, standing above the quay with its black roof, slowly comes closer. It is regarded as the oldest stone-built house in the country and was designed by Nicolai Eigtved, architect to the Danish royal court. Skúli Magnússon, the first Icelander to hold the office of sheriff, commissioned it to serve as his private house between 1752 and 1755.

After his lifetime, other influential people, including Governor Ólafur Stephensen and his son Magnús Stephensen, chief judge at the supreme court, resided in the Viðey House. The latter had progressive ideas, and operated the only printing press in Iceland on Viðey from 1819 to 1844.

In the early 20th century the island prospered from the fishing industry, and in the following years up to 140 people settled here. After the closure of the fish factory, the employees' families returned to the mainland, and by the 1950s only a few farmers remained.

Caraway plants, a survival from Skúli Magnússon's agricultural experiments, still grow on the meadows of the island. After his death in 1794, Magnússon was buried in the church next to the Viðey House. It was built from basalt, a stone that is quarried on the island, and is the second-oldest church in Iceland. Its original furnishings, the oldest church furnishings in the country, remain. As women once sat separately from the men in church, the pews on the left, seen from the entrance, are seven centimetres lower.

The island of Viðey consists of two parts, Heimaey and Vesturey. They are connected by a man-made piece of land, Eiðið. It is possible to spend the whole day walking the trails on the small island – just be sure not to miss the last ferry back to the mainland in the evening.

Address Skarfagarðar (ferry terminal for Viðey), 104 Reykjavík | **Getting there** Bus 12
to Dalbraut or 16 to Heðinsgata, then walk to Skarfagarðar via Heðinsgata and Klettagarðar;
towards the city centre on routes 49 and 41, then turn right into Klettagarðar 1.7 kilo-
metres after the Kleppsspítali hospital, and left into Skarfagarðar | **Hours** Ferry timetable:
www.videy.com | **Tip** Richard Serra's work of art *Milestones* on Vesturey consists of nine
pairs of basalt columns that have been placed around the island.

95_ The Ylströnd

A swim in the lukewarm North Atlantic

Geothermal water is not in short supply in Iceland, so it is not surprising to find a bay for swimmers where the sea is warmed up with hot water. In Nauthólsvík at the foot of the hill Öskjuhlíð, hot water flows into a lagoon that is divided from the North Atlantic by a stone wall. Here is Ylströnd, a man-made beach with light-coloured sand.

If you expect to find lukewarm water for bathing here, first of all reconsider your personal definition of 'lukewarm' before you plunge in. The water in the lagoon reaches a temperature between 15 and 19 degrees Celsius and no more, even in summer. In winter the inflow of hot water makes hardly any difference at all, and so a bracing 4 to 6 degrees Celsius awaits the hardy swimmer. For Icelanders, however, low temperatures are seldom a reason for refraining from an activity, and they enjoy a swim wearing gloves of neoprene rubber and a cosy woolly hat. Anyway, swimming in cold water is said to promote a sense of well-being. Whether they are frozen to the marrow or not, at all times of the year swimmers can take advantage of a pool several metres long heated to a temperature of 38 degrees Celsius. It is immediately above the beach, next to the changing rooms, and is used for warming up or simply as a place to relax.

The beach on Nauthólsvík opened in 2000, and a year later the hot showers, a kiosk and a steam bath were installed. More than 500,000 visitors per year now come to swim here, and on the few summer days when it gets properly warm, the Ylströnd beach can be genuinely crowded.

The bay takes its name from the Nauthóll farm. Following a typhus epidemic in the early 20th century, all the houses were burned. Its remains can be seen to the north of the car park. These bad old days are now long gone, and Ylströnd has become one of three beaches in Iceland to gain a Blue Flag award for good quality.

Address Nauthólsvegur, 101 Reykjavík | Getting there Bus 5 to Nauthólsvík – HR; by car: take route 49 towards the city centre, then turn left after 7 kilometres onto Nauthólsvegur and follow the signs | Hours 15 May – 15 Aug daily 10am – 7pm, 16 Aug – 14 May Mon – Fri 11am – 1pm, Mon & Wed also 5 – 7pm, Sat 11am – 3pm | Tip Only a few metres west of the beach in an elevated position are four outsized wooden chairs on which you can sit to enjoy the view across to the other side of Nauthólsvík.

96 Bobby Fischer's Grave
The last resting place of an eccentric chess genius

Only the chess pieces reveal that one of the best chess players of all time lies beneath the gravestone in front of the church of Laugardælir near Selfoss. The American grandmaster Bobby Fischer spent the last years of his life in Iceland, where he became world champion in 1972. In the 'match of the century' he defeated the Soviet grandmaster Boris Spassky. This was not merely a sporting duel between two chess players. The series also symbolised the conflict between the two superpowers in the Cold War. In a dramatic contest, Fischer finally defeated Spassky by 12½ points to 8½.

Fischer's greatest triumph simultaneously marked the end of his career. He was not willing to meet Anatoly Karpov in 1975 to defend his title. It was not until 20 years later that Fischer reappeared in the world of chess, winning for a second time against Spassky during the Balkan conflict in Yugoslavia. By playing there, Fischer knowingly contravened sanctions imposed by the US government, and never again returned to his homeland for fear of being prosecuted. He lived in Hungary, in Japan and in the Philippines – always afraid that the American secret service would take him back to the USA.

In July 2004 he was placed under arrest when he attempted to board a flight from Japan to Manila with an invalid passport. A group of old friends from Iceland made efforts to secure his release, and on 22 March, 2005 the Icelandic parliament granted him full citizenship for humanitarian reasons. Two days later, Bobby Fischer returned to Iceland. After his death on 17 January, 2008, he was laid to rest in Laugardælir. However, in the course of a paternity suit, his body was exhumed in 2010 to take a sample of his DNA. A previous acquaintance named Marilyn Young asserted that Bobby Fischer was the father of her daughter. The results of the test contradicted her claim.

ROBERT JAMES
FISCHER

F. 9. MARS 1943
D. 17. JANÚAR 2008

Address Laugardælir, 800 Selfoss | Getting there From Reykjavík via Ring Road 1 to
Selfoss, following the Ring Road and turning off left towards Laugardælir (golf course)
just before reaching Selfoss | Tip The Bobby Fischer Center in Selfoss has a thorough
documentation of Fischer's story. Guided tours reveal strange details about the 'match of
the century' and convey an impression of Fischer's eccentric personality (Austurvegur 21,
800 Selfoss).

97__The Luxury Adventure Hotel

Holiday by the power station

At the edge of the Þingvellir National Park, a UNESCO World Heritage site only one hour by car from Reykjavík, the long building of the ION luxury and adventure hotel nestles into a field of lava. Its narrow façade rests on concrete pillars, and behind a large frontage of glass lies the Northern Lights Bar.

In 2011 Sigurlaug Sverrisdóttir bought a building that had served as accommodation for employees of the Nesjavellir geothermal power station, and made her vision of a luxury hotel in Iceland's rough landscape a reality. On account of the hot springs that run beneath the hotel at a depth of only a few metres, the structure had to be designed to be seven times more robust than would have been necessary in Reykjavík. At the same time, these springs supply hot thermal water to the 10-metre-long outdoor pool of the spa, where guests can relax after walking across a glacier or taking a kayak trip.

In the hotel interior, the designers opted for natural materials such as driftwood, lava and Icelandic herbs. They recycled car tyres for the wash basins and made both beds and chairs from re-usable materials. The hotel has already won several awards for its environmentally friendly Nordic design. Yet these awards cannot entirely cancel out the effect of the steaming geothermal plant of Nesjavellir 900 metres away. 'Some guests feel disturbed by it,' says Katrín Ósk Sigurgeirsdóttir, the hotel manager. 'But when we explain to them that we could not use green energy or geothermal water without the power station, they understand our link to it and to the surroundings.' The view from the Northern Lights Bar is appreciated much more. Through the panorama windows guests can watch the aurora borealis in winter, while enjoying a drink in elegant surroundings and in a warm atmosphere.

Address On Grafningsvegur Efri near the turn-off to route 435, about 36 kilometres north-west of Selfoss; Nesjavellir on Þingvallavatn, 801 Selfoss | **Getting there** Route 36 towards Þingvellir, then continue on the 360 towards Nesjavellir and follow the signs to the power station | **Tip** A few hundred metres from the hotel is a climbing course, open from May to September. It has 50 climbing points and a zip wire 85 metres long.

98__ The Silfra Fissure
Paradise for tough divers

For so-called cocktail divers, who like to explore the seas in warm water, the Silfra Fissure is not the ideal spot. 'All year round the water temperature is around 2 to 4 degrees Celsius,' says David Ramsay, an Englishman whose company Magma Dive organises tours for divers. 'But if you want to see some of the clearest water in the world, the Þingvellir National Park is just right.'

The Silfra Fissure is part of Lake Þingvallavatn and is situated at the divide where the Eurasian and North American continental plates are drifting apart. However, David does not try to nurture the illusion of a dive between the continents: 'The rift zone between the tectonic plates is much larger than the narrow Silfra Fissure.' Nevertheless, this diving site has unique characteristics. Electric blue, fiery red, intense green, but all of it somehow soft,' is how David describes the underwater world there.

On a car park near Lake Silfra, Sarah and Gareth, whose home is near Cambridge in England, put on their heavy diving gear. It takes them about half an hour to wriggle into their suits and heated jackets. Special gloves keep their hands dry and as warm as possible below the water surface. 'Your fingers start to shiver after about 30 minutes, and then you no longer feel very comfortable under the water,' explains David, who once dived at Siltra with the Hollywood star Tom Cruise.

Those who are willing to take these side-effects of the dive into account can have a unique experience in the Silfra Fissure. 'The visibility through the clear water is unbelievable. I have never seen rocks and caves like this anywhere – and then the colours!' Sarah comments enthusiastically, and makes her way to the ladder that is the point of entry for the Silfra dive.

Experienced divers can descend to depths of 60 metres in the fissure. After that they prefer a hot cup of tea to a cocktail.

Address Vallarvegur, Þingvellir Nationalpark, about 43 kilometres north of 801 Selfoss, www.magmadive.is | Getting there Take route 36 to the national park information centre in the north of Þingvallavatn and turn onto route 361 there | Hours Always open | Tip There are several beautiful walking trails around the Silfra Fissure, passing the Þingvellir church, the Öxarárfoss waterfall and various viewing points where you can look across the plain where the Alþingi, the predecessor of the Icelandic parliament, first met in AD 930.

99_Grottá

A leisure island with a family tradition

Take a look at the tide tables before you set off for Grottá, the lighthouse island. It is situated off the Seltjarnarnes peninsula, not far from Reykjavík, and can only be reached at low tide. At high tide, the ocean water covers the narrow connecting causeway and cuts off this terrain from the mainland. This was not always the situation: on 9 January, 1788, a violent flood carried away a sizeable piece of land and destroyed the permanent access route to Grottá.

The first mention of Grottá in historic documents dates back to the 16th century. It is believed, however, that the peninsula was settled and used for agriculture much earlier than that. In the first half of the 19th century, Grottá had been abandoned.

Later in that century fishermen and boat builders settled here, and in 1897 the first lighthouse was built. Þorvarð Einarsson worked as lighthouse keeper until 1931. After his death, his son Albert Þorvarðarson took on the task for almost 40 years until he drowned in 1970. The present-day lighthouse was built during his term of office. Its beams first guided ships safely around the promontory in November 1947. A memorial plaque on Grottá honours the two lighthouse keepers.

The structure is now owned by the local authority of Seltjarnarnes. Both its immediate surroundings and the adjacent meadows on the mainland have been declared a nature reserve. The birds that breed on the coast and the nearby lake called Bakkatjörn include glaucous gulls, red-breasted mergansers, ruddy turnstones and cormorants. Various kinds of seaweed, mussels and plants such as Arctic sea rocket and sea chickweed also grow here. In summer, access to Grottá is prohibited at times so that the birds are not disturbed, but in the breeding season and during the hours of high tide, you can still enjoy a fine view of this idyllic island from the mainland.

Address Norðurströnd, 170 Seltjarnarnes | **Getting there** Bus 11 to Hofgarðar, then walk to Grottá via Lindarbraut and Norðurströnd; by car: Ring Road 1, then route 49 towards Reykjavík to its end, turn left at the roundabout into Eiðsgrandi; its continuation is Norðurströnd | **Hours** Closed from May to 15 July | **Tip** About 350 metres from Grottá is a geothermal bath, probably the smallest in Iceland. Since 2005 this basalt basin measuring two by two metres between the stones of the coastal embankment has been available for soaking your feet in the water of a hot spring with a lovely view.

100__ Tvísöngur

A monument to song

It looks like a futuristic shelter for walkers, but is in fact a sound installation called *Tvísöngur*. Its five grey concrete domes stand in a pretty location above the town of Seyðisfjörður, on the slopes of the fjord of the same name in the east of Iceland. They are a tangible representation of the traditional Icelandic art of tvísöngur ('twin-song'), which is based on five-tone harmony. The idea for these unusual structures derives from a German artist, Lukas Kühne, who had already visualised the chromatic scale in a concrete installation in Tallinn, the capital of Estonia.

He built *Tvísöngur* in 2012 in collaboration with the German cultural institute (Goethe-Institut) in Denmark, with Skaftfell, the Center for Visual Art in Seyðisfjörður and with the local government. In five and a half weeks the domes, two to four metres in height, were constructed. They are connected with each other and cover an area of about 30 square metres. Each of the five spaces is allocated to one of the tones of twin-song, and the architecture of the domes works as an amplifier when someone sings or plays music inside.

The remoteness of the site is deliberate, as tranquillity is required for experimenting with sounds or music. It is easier to let go and be uninhibited when no one is listening. Trying things out is part of the idea, as you do not need to understand the fundamentals of five-tone harmony for this experience. There are no instructions. The purpose is to feel how the sound changes in different spaces, whether from an instrument or a voice.

Lukas Kühne's *Tvísöngur* has given Icelandic twin-song a specific site in the world, but for the people of Seyðisfjörður his concrete sculpture is much more. On this small space on the hill above the town they can make music, enjoy the peace, hold a party or take shelter from the rain – *Tvísöngur* makes all of this possible.

Address Hafnargata, 710 Seyðisfjörður | Getting there Via route 93 to Seyðisfjörður, turn right onto Austurvegur, straight on to Hafnargata until you see a small car park on the right | Hours Always open | Tip On the Fjarðarheiði plateau between Seyðisfjörður and Egilsstaðir is a beautiful lake, Heiðarvatn. Its water is deep blue, and ice floes can float on the surface even in summer. On route 93 above and below the lake there are places to stop a car.

101__ The Field of Lupins
A divisive plant

In Iceland, the lupin has had a meteoric career that many people now view sceptically. In the summer months, this plant from the legume family flowers all around the island, except in the highland regions. Especially along the Ring Road in the south, lupins have taken possession of large areas, but in many other parts of the country, too, thousands of plants from this hardy species cover entire slopes of the hills and colour them blue. Flower lovers, walkers and tourists may appreciate the sight, but environmentalists have come to regard the lupin as a pest, as with its height of up to 120 centimetres, it crowds out every other kind of vegetation.

In the mid-20th century the lupin was purposely planted in Iceland as a measure against ground erosion. According to Landgræðsla ríkisins, the official body for protecting the ground, more than 35 per cent of Iceland is barren wilderness. This resulted from forest clearance, climate change and volcanic eruptions in past centuries. The plan was that the lupin, with its strong roots, would prevent light and loose soils from being swept away by the wind, leaving behind nothing but infertile wasteland.

The plant fulfilled its task – but in consequence also spread out like an alien invader. It could be said that the people of Iceland are now divided into two parties: the supporters of the lupin love it as an attractive flower in gardens and parks, while farmers use it as an intermediate crop to fertilise their fields, as lupins add the nutrient nitrogen to the soil. The opponents of the plant include environmentalists who regard the uncontrollable spread of lupins as a threat to many native plant species. It is difficult to keep the lupins in check, and in this case Icelanders cannot rely on their ever-hungry sheep to control them: bitter substances in the plant mean that the sheep simply don't like to eat it.

Address On Ring Road 1, 861 Skógar, for example | **Getting there** Via Ring Road 1 towards Vík; the field of lupins is about 3 kilometres east of Skógar | **Hours** They flower between May and early August, depending on the temperature. | **Tip** You can easily collect lupin seeds from the pods to plant at home after the lupins have flowered (they look like pea pods, but don't eat them: lupin seeds are poisonous!).

102 — The Ölkelda Spring
Mineral water straight from the ground

On the Snæfellsnes peninsula, only a few hundred metres from route 54, a dripping pipe rises out of the ground next to a farmhouse. It looks like a superannuated hydrant, but on closer inspection turns out to be the Ölkelda spring. It was discovered in the mid-18th century and fitted up more or less as it appears today in 1904 by the farmer Gísli Þórðarson.

An information panel next to the Ölkelda spring records an analysis of the water. In comparison with normal drinking water, this report attests that the spring has a much higher concentration of elements with beneficial health effects: calcium, chloride, sodium, iron, potassium and magnesium.

This investigation was carried out in 1972 and is therefore not right up to date. At that time, the water was found to have positive effects for heart and kidney complaints, as well as for diabetes. Drinking the water of Ölkelda is also said to be good for the teeth and blood. Who knows whether this still holds true? However, for decades the farmers of this district have sworn by the health-giving properties of the water.

If you take a thorough look at the chemical analysis, the high levels of iron are noticeable. This is also the explanation of the reddish-brown colour of the ground around the spring. Compared with normal tap water from the public supply, that from the Ölkelda spring has an iron content one thousand times as high. Any who venture to drink from it will taste this. It has a rusty finish, and the natural carbon dioxide sparkles surprisingly on the palate. The high mineral content means that the water is slightly cloudy. If this does not bother you and you find the taste acceptable, then go ahead and do the same as the local farmers: fill up a bottle with the spring water. The method of payment is simple and typical for Iceland: place the money in the wooden box.

Address Snæfellsnesvegur, 356 Snæfellsbær | Getting there From Borgarnes take route 54, go straight ahead at the turn-off for Stykkishólmur, then right to the spring after 12.8 kilometres at the sign 'Ölkelda' | Hours Always open | Tip About 21 kilometres further towards Ólafsvík, route 5720 forks right to the Kálfárvellir farm, where two waterfalls that flow into the river Kálfá can be seen.

103 Bjarnarhöfn

Rotten meat from the Greenland shark

People have always displayed a lot of imagination where the preparation of food is concerned. How else could you explain the fact that Icelanders leave shark meat, which ought to be inedible, in the ground to rot for weeks, before drying and then eating it? This is a traditional method of curing shark meat in Iceland, especially at Bjarnarhöfn. For generations, the family of Hildibrandur Bjarnason has produced 'hákarl', a delicacy with a pungent taste that is made from the meat of the Greenland shark. In summer, visitors are unlikely to witness the preparation of one of these fish. They weigh between 600 and 800 kilograms, and are mainly hunted in winter, sometimes in spring. At this time of the year they appear in layers of warmer water off Greenland and thus come within range of the fishing boats.

At Bjarnarhöfn the Greenland sharks, which are four to five metres long, are cut up into chunks the size of a loaf of bread. Packed in wooden boxes with holes to let in air, the wobbly lumps are stored for about six weeks in a cool place – of which there is no shortage in Iceland in winter. In the old days they used to bury the meat in the ground, but this method of storage is no longer practised at Bjarnarhöfn. After this period in cold storage, the pieces of shark meat are taken to the drying house, where after three to four months the urea in the meat has been converted to ammonia and has evaporated. Visitors who enter the drying house will have this confirmed by their nose. A harmful substance called trimethylamine nitrogen oxide is also removed during this process, and the hákarl is ready to eat. If you do not find all of this too off-putting, you can of course try a piece of 'rotted shark' at Bjarnarhöfn and view a small exhibition about the history of processing shark meat – assuming that the highly intense taste of the hákarl hasn't knocked you out.

Address Bjarnarhöfn, 340 Stykkishólmur | Getting there From Stykkishólmur take route 54 towards Grundarfjördur, then turn right onto route 577 towards Helgafellssveit and after 2 kilometres go left, following the sign to Bjarnarhöfn; the farm is about 25 kilometres south-west of Stykkishólmur | Hours Daily 9am–6pm | Tip The wooden church below Bjarnahöfn, easily reached on foot, is one of the oldest in the country, built between 1856 and 1859.

104__Hafnargata
Where Ben Stiller took off

Hollywood likes Iceland – and this long pre-dates the high praise showered on the island by the American actor Ben Stiller. In 2012, he filmed parts of the movie *The Secret Life of Walter Mitty* in Iceland. One of the locations for the filming was Hafnargata in beautiful Stykkishólmur. Walter Mitty, alias Ben Stiller, stormed spontaneously out of a bar to leap into a helicopter that was already taking off. 'To shoot the scene, they even painted the town hall of Stykkishólmur dark grey,' recalls Leifur B. Dagfinnsson. He is a co-founder of the film company called Truenorth that handles many movie productions in Iceland. The monument on the square by the harbour was also given a different appearance for the film.

The town hall is now resplendent again in a pale shade of beige, while books and toys are on sale in what was supposedly a bar. 'On the whole, the people at the film locations give us excellent support,' says Leifur. 'They know that our big production teams are a source of good business for the restaurants, bars and shops.' And this business carries on even after the film teams have left the scene. Leifur B. Dagfinnsson is convinced that Walter Mitty, for example, has made a significant contribution to the large numbers of tourists coming to Iceland in recent years. 'Our country isn't just an anonymous film location – it plays a role in the movie itself. That means publicity for Iceland that has an effect for years.'

This kind of publicity is no longer needed to attract directors and producers such as Ridley Scott, Clint Eastwood or Christopher Nolan. They were long ago won over by the light conditions, the professional film teams and the beauty of Iceland's scenery. We can expect that in the years to come, too, heroes of the big screen will be knocking around with the glaciers, lava fields and waterfalls of Iceland as a backdrop.

Address Hafnargata, 340 Stykkishólmur | Getting there Via routes 54 and 58 to
Stykkishólmur, then straight ahead on Aðalgata until the road turns off left into Hafnargata |
Tip In the helicopter scene, a red wooden house with a large number of windows can be seen.
This is the Egilsenshús at Aðalgata 2, built in 1867 and now a hotel.

105 The Library of Water

Glacier water ... not for borrowing

In its first incarnation, the white building on a rock above Stykkishólmur was already used as a library. In those days, however, the entries in the catalogue were books printed on paper – not glass cylinders, each filled with about 200 litres of water that is thousands of years old. The water comes from the ice of 24 Icelandic glaciers, including Snæfellsjökull, Köldukvíslarjökull and the famous Eyjafjallajökull. The idea for this unusual installation entitled *Water, selected* derives from the American artist Roni Horn. In 2006 and 2007 she drove off again and again with assistants to cut blocks of ice out of the glaciers with a power saw. They collected the melted water in canisters and later poured it into the three-metre-high glass cylinders. Since then it has cast reflections of light onto the specially made floor around the columns of water.

The flooring of vulcanised rubber is part of Horn's artwork *You are the weather (Iceland)*. She has printed adjectives connected with the weather on it. English and Icelandic words such as 'windy', 'foggy', 'frískandi' and 'dyntótt' can be read. The intention is to arouse visitors' personal associations with weather.

Roni Horn has a great artistic interest in the subject of weather. For her work *Weather reports you* she conducted interviews with people from Stykkishólmur and its surroundings in 2005 and 2006. This resulted not only in general descriptions of sun, wind and snow, but also in highly personal stories about the perception of weather. The records of these conversations can be seen in a room next to the Library of Water.

The atmosphere in the library is subdued, as if the glass cylinders could be broken by excessive noise. They probably have a longer life expectation than the glaciers, which are threatened by climate change and may soon only be visible in liquid form in the Library of Water.

Address Bókhlöðustígur 17, 340 Stykkishólmur, vatnasan@gmail.com | Getting there Via routes 54 and 58 to Stykkishólmur, turn left into Silfurgata after the second petrol station, then right, left and right again onto Bókhlöðustígur | Hours June – Aug daily 11am – 5pm, Sept – May by arrangement Thu – Sat 11am – 5pm | Tip Opposite, by the harbour, a tall rock rises from the water. On this rock a red lighthouse marks the harbour entrance of Stykkishólmur. You can explore the rock on little paths, with enchanting views.

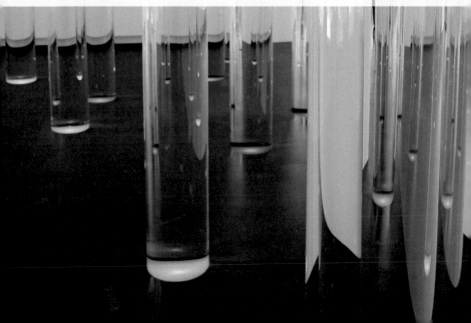

106 Dyrhólaey

A crumbling doorway in southern Iceland

If you would like to unlock the secrets of this volcanic island in the North Atlantic, take a look through Iceland's 'doorway'. This is a hole in a headland 120 metres high called Dyrhólaey, which translates as 'door-hole island'. It juts into the sea near Vík í Myrdal, forming one of the southernmost points in Iceland. Dyrhólaey and the rocky islets close to it were created about 80,000 years ago by a volcanic eruption beneath the sea. With stoical inevitability, over the ages the sea washed the softer layers of stone from the tip of the headland until the 'doorway' had been carved out. It is so large that sailing boats can easily pass through. A dare-devil pilot is said to have flown a light aircraft through the gap in the rock.

Some way to the west of Dyrhólaey stands an old lighthouse dating from 1927. This white concrete structure with a red lamp on the roof is about 13 metres high and looks a little bit like a medieval fortress – although it is now a luxury hotel. From there, a walking trail leads to the tip of Dyrhólaey. This is not, however, entirely without risk, as in May 2015 a large piece of the cliffs broke away from the mainland and plunged into the ocean – taking a section of the walking trail with it.

From the tip of the headland you have a spectacular view of the sea, the coast and the Mýrdalsjökull glacier in the hinterland. The 'doorway' is not visible, of course, as you are standing above it. If you would like to take a photograph of it, the best course is to go to a cliff further east, which can easily be reached by road.

Since 1978 the Dyrhólaey promontory has been a protected nature reserve. It is a breeding area for various kinds of sea bird, including fulmars, puffins and eider ducks. To allow the birds to hatch and raise their offspring, it is possible that access to Dyrhólaey is restricted or prohibited between 1 May and 25 June.

Address Dyrhólavegur, 870 Vík | Getting there Ring Road 1, turn onto route 218 at Vík, Dyrhólaey is about 19 kilometres west of Vík | Hours May be closed between May and 25 June | Tip On the cliff east of Dyrhólaey, a path leads to Kirkjufjara beach, a good place for a walk (watch out for waves and tides!) where fine columns of basalt can be seen.

107 __ Reynisfjara
Smooth stones, a geometrical cave and petrified trolls

Between the mountain Reynisfjall and the Dyrhólaey peninsula in the south of Iceland lies Reynisfjara, a lava beach three kilometres long. It is known for its pebbles, smoothed by the water to round shapes with a colour ranging from dark grey to deep black when the waves wash over them. Wherever you look on Reynisfjara, at every point of the compass there is something to discover.

At the east end of the beach, the sea has carved the Hálsanefshellir cave out of the rock. In the cave roof the basalt columns, often hexagonal, that are formed when hot lava cools can be seen with wonderful clarity. Outside the cave, too, these rock formations stand in rows on the mountain wall like organ pipes.

In front of Hálsanefshellir, three rocks, up to 66 metres high, emerge from the sea. They are called Skessudrangar, Langhamar and Landdrangur. According to a legend they are two petrified trolls who tried to pull to shore a three-masted ship that had run aground. At the break of day, the sun turned the trolls to stone, and the ship was petrified with them. Further inland, immediately behind the beach, is the Dyrhólaós lagoon, which is supplied with the water from several rivers. The marshy area around the lagoon is used by many native bird species and by migrating birds in their passage as a place to rest, a nesting site and a source of food.

The western end of the beach is formed by Arnardranga – the eagle rock. Great birds of prey can no longer be found here. Other species, sea birds, have taken over the rock as a breeding ground, but the old name has survived. Although Reynisfjara beach looks lovely, it is also dangerous, not only for trolls who shun the sunlight. Again and again, treacherous waves have taken walkers on the beach by surprise and swept them into the sea. Usually they escaped with just a fright, but there was not always a happy ending.

Address Reynishverfisvegur, 870 Vík | Getting there From Ring Road 1 turn off at Vík onto route 215 | Tip Between Reynisfjara and Vík lies the mountain Reynisfjall. On its south-east side, facing the village, in most years many puffins breed and can be observed from the beach.

108_ The Wrecked Aircraft
Emergency landing on Sólheimasandur

The pilot of a US Navy Douglas DC-3 showed his skill in November 1973, when he had to make an emergency landing with the propeller aircraft in Sólheimarsandur due to technical problems. All seven passengers survived, and the desert of grey sand on the south coast of Iceland fortunately became a graveyard for the plane only, not for its crew. More than 40 years later, the wreck of the DC-3 is still in remarkably good condition, even though the entire interior fittings, the engines and the wings are missing. For photographers, the scene is nevertheless a real gift: a silver aircraft on grey sand, its nose pointing up to the sky as if it wanted to take off again. All around there is nothing but desert, and not far away the waves of the North Atlantic crash on the shore.

Between Vík í Mýrdal and the Skogafoss waterfall the path leading to the wreck of the Douglas forks off from the Ring Road. Only a small sign saying 'Flugvélaflak (DC3)' indicates the spot where the emergency landing took place. With or without a four-wheel-drive vehicle, visitors bump across the track, which is marked by stones and wooden posts. Many are reluctant to set out on this four-kilometre hike through the sandy wilderness. It takes a good hour, but is a worthwhile experience. When the sun is shining, the air above the hilly sand shimmers and refracts, and it is almost impossible to estimate distances. You feel a bit lost until the wreck of the DC-3 finally appears.

From this moment, photo fans can no longer hold back, and their fingers scarcely leave the shutter button: overall views, close-ups, details, selfies. When the memory card is full with pictures of the DC-3, all that remains for walkers is the rough return journey. Drivers get into their cars and watch the wrecked plane getting smaller and smaller in their rear-view mirror until it disappears behind a grey sand dune.

Address Þjóðvegur, 871 Vík | Getting there Ring Road 1 to a track 24 kilometres west of Vík and 2 kilometres east of the turn-off to route 221, then follow the wooden posts | Tip East of Sólheimasandur is Pétursey, a hill of tufa with a good view of the Mýrdalsjökull glacier. Route 219 goes all round the 275-metre hill, and a nice walking trail starts from the west side of Pétursey.

109_ The Old Metal Shop

Cutting, drilling and forging as in bygone days

Lots and lots of oil for lubrication has always been the recipe for maintaining the ageing machines in the historic metalwork shop in Þingeyri. When you enter, you can smell this straight away. In the old days the lathes, cutting tools and drills were always oiled at the end of the working week. Today, they are lubricated according to their hours of operation. These are noted down by Þórir Örn Guðmundsson, who looks after the old workshop. He gives tours for visitors and shows them how the work was done in past times. 'In 1913 Guðmundur J. Sigurðsson set up the workshop. It was one of the first in Iceland. In its most prosperous years, eight to ten people were employed here,' he explains.

Back then, iron was often cast by hand to make components for fishing boats. The required parts included rollers that made it easier to pull in the heavy nets, and a kind of power steering for ships. 'The son of the workshop owner devised this system himself. It was then possible for one man to handle the wheel alone and steer the boat.'

Since 1995 the workshop has no longer been in normal operation, but it remains open for visitors. With a little luck they can see the old machines being used, as spare parts for fishing boats are occasionally produced. A few times a year Þórir Örn also heats up the smelting oven in order to cast iron. 'The sand mould boxes and the rest of the old equipment are still in wonderful working order,' he says with pride. This also applies to the lathes and cutting tools, which are powered via leather or textile belts attached to the ceiling of the workshop. A large diesel engine drove the belts until 1951, when it was replaced by an electric motor. 'The most recent machine in the metal workshop dates from the same decade, from 1958. It is a lathe, and it's the only one of the machines that was given a name.' Þórir Örn grins: 'The new one!'

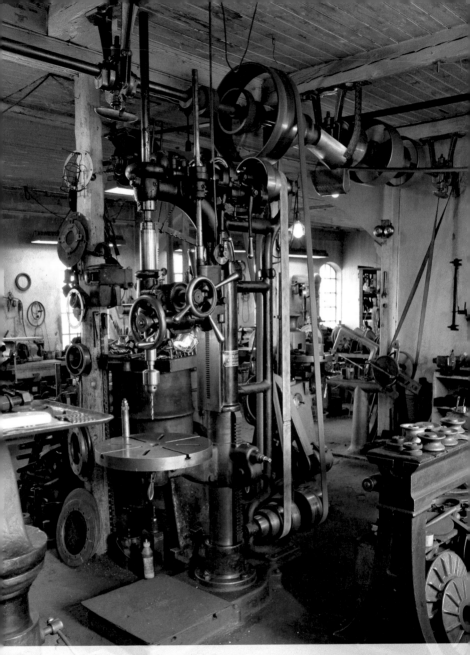

Address Hafnarstræti, 470 Þingeyri | Getting there Via route 60 to Þingeyri, in the town follow Fjarðargata and its continuation Hafnarstræti, where the workshop is on the right | Hours 15 May – 15 Sept daily 9am – 6pm | Tip Café Simbahöllin occupies an old grocer's shop on Fjarðargata. The owners specialise in Belgian waffles with cream and rhubarb jam (open June – Aug).

110 The Strandarkirkja
Where a divine angel acted as a lighthouse

Only a few metres behind a stone embankment on the south coast of Iceland, where the waves of the North Atlantic break with undiminished force on the beach, stands the grey Strandarkirkja. This wooden church, almost 12 metres long, was built in 1887–1888 on a small rise that is surrounded by a stone wall. Inside the Strandarkirkja, visitors can take a seat on the brown wooden benches. If it gets crowded inside, for example when concerts are held after the church service in summer, the gallery can also be used. The walls are painted salmon-pink and harmonise with the light blue ceiling, which has been lovingly decorated with golden stars.

To the west of Þorlákshöfn, where the Strandarkirkja stands today, there is thought to have been a church from the 11th or 12th century onwards. Various stories are told to explain why it was constructed here, in such a remote spot. According to one of these tales, during a stormy night a boat loaded with timber lost its way off this coast. The sailors feared for their lives and prayed, asking God to spare them. They promised they would use the wood to build a church at the place where they reached land alive. Suddenly they spotted a bright light and headed for it. When they gained the shore, the sailors realised that the source of the light was a radiant angel. They kept their promise and built a church, which was one of the best-endowed in Iceland for a long time. People from all over the country donated money in the hope that their prayers, too, would be heard.

A sculpture entitled *Landsýn* (Land in Sight) by the artist Gunnfríður Jónsdóttir, who is buried in the cemetery of the Strandarkirkja, commemorates the rescue of the sailors. Her statue was erected not far away in 1950. It depicts a nun – not holding a flashlight, but with a small cross in her left hand.

Address Selvogur near Suðurstrandarvegur, 815 Þorlákshöfn | Getting there Via Ring
Road 1 and route 39 to Þorlákshöfn, then right at the roundabout onto route 427 towards
Grindavík and left to the Strandarkirkja after 14.5 kilometres | Hours Summer daily from
9am until the evening mealtime | Tip On the gravel track to the Strandarkirkja is a snack
bar serving sausages, where you can also get a good cup of coffee or cocoa. A small building
next to it houses a flea market in summer.

111__ Ytra Lón Hostel

From construction containers to rooms for guests

The distance between Reykjavík and the small Ytra Lón hostel on the Langanes peninsula in the north-east of Iceland is almost 400 kilometres as the crow flies. It is difficult to find accommodation further from the bustle of the island capital unless you want to spend your nights in a tent or a campervan.

Mirjam Blekkenhorst, who moved from Grímsstaðir to Ytra Lón in 1991 with her husband Sverrir and 300 sheep, likes this remoteness. To start with this Dutch-Icelandic couple only ran the farm, and then in 1998 they opened the hostel.

Langanes is known for its wealth of bird life, with gannets, terns and eider ducks. Long walking routes to the best spots for watching birds attract ornithologists to this lonely area. They can get a good night's sleep in one of the 16 rooms at Ytra Lón. In 2010 Mirjam and Sverrir extended the hostel when they were able to buy for a bargain price several container structures that had been used to accommodate German engineers during construction work on the Kárahnjúkar Dam. The feel of a building site has given way to a cosy farm atmosphere, even though the functionally equipped rooms cannot deny their origin. This is something that does not bother Frank Edna Calenda from Florida in the least. In contrast to his last stay on the Langanes peninsula almost 50 years ago, this is pure luxury. In 1967 he spent a year with the US Air Force on a military base on the nearby mountain Heiðarfjall. 'The winter was snowy, cold and lonely,' he recalls, but he returned with his wife to the place where he served. 'At that time our only contact was via audio-tapes that were sent to and fro between Iceland and America.'

Twenty-three years after Frank Edna Calenda's time in the US Air Force, Mirjam and Sverrir came to Langanes and now offer their guests all they can hope for from a holiday stay on a farm.

Address Langanesvegur, 681 Þórshöfn | **Getting there** Route 85 towards Þórshöfn, pass through the village and continue on route 869; the path to the hostel branches off 9 kilometres beyond the new airport | **Hours** All year | **Tip** At the northernmost tip of the Langanes peninsula, the bird rock Stóri-Karl rises from the sea in front of the Skoruvík cliffs. It is one of the main breeding grounds in Iceland for gannets. The Járnkarl viewing platform was built on the cliffs so that bird-watchers can observe the gannets without getting into danger.

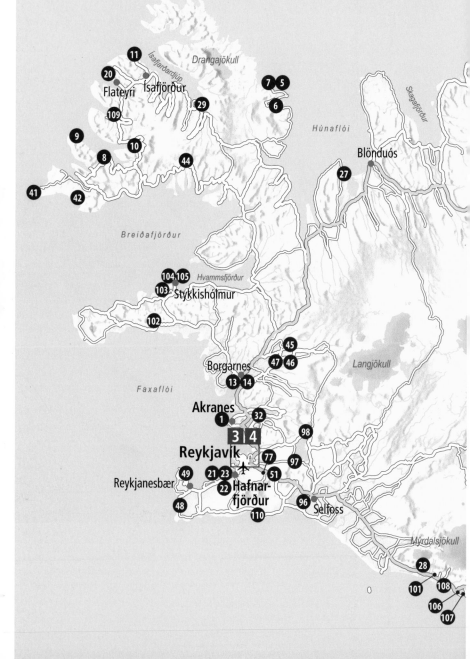

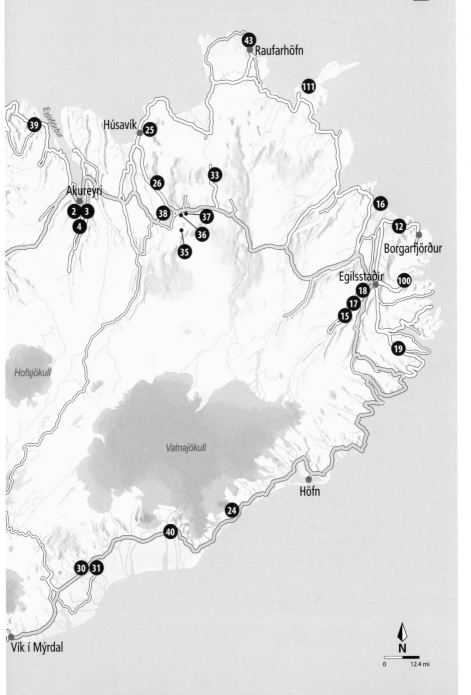

2

Raufarhöfn

43

111

Húsavík

25

39

Eyjafjörður

26

33

Akureyri

16

2 3

38

37

12

4

36

Borgarfjörður

35

Egilsstaðir

100

18

17

15

19

Hofsjökull

Vatnajökull

Höfn

24

40

30 31

Vík í Mýrdal

N

0   12.4 mi

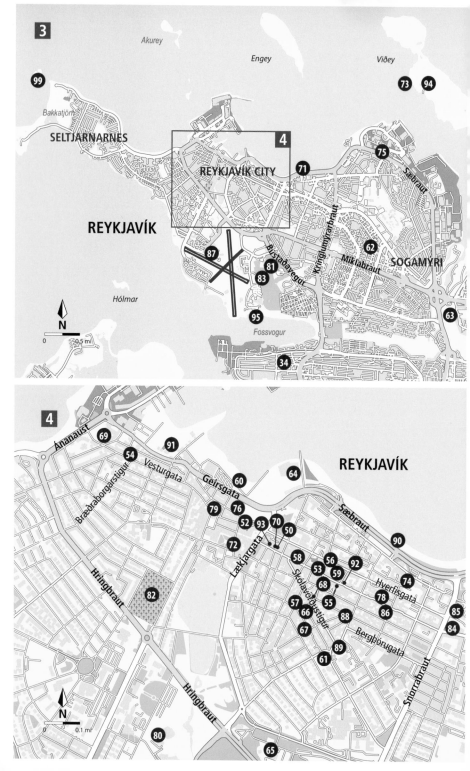

Lucia Jay von Seldeneck,
Carolin Huder, Verena Eidel
111 PLACES IN BERLIN
THAT YOU SHOULDN'T MISS
ISBN 978-3-95451-208-9

Rüdiger Liedtke
111 PLACES IN MUNICH
THAT YOU SHOULDN'T MISS
ISBN 978-3-95451-222-5

Rike Wolf
111 PLACES IN HAMBURG
THAT YOU SHOULDN'T MISS
ISBN 978-3-95451-234-8

Paul Kohl
111 PLACES IN BERLIN
ON THE TRAIL OF THE NAZIS
ISBN 978-3-95451-323-9

Sharon Fernandes
111 PLACES IN NEW DELHI
THAT YOU MUST NOT MISS
ISBN 978-3-95451-648-3

Sally Asher, Michael Murphy
111 PLACES IN NEW ORLEANS
THAT YOU MUST NOT MISS
ISBN 978-3-95451-645-2

Dirk Engelhardt
111 PLACES IN BARCELONA
THAT YOU MUST NOT MISS
ISBN 978-3-95451-353-6

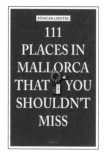

Rüdiger Liedtke
111 PLACES ON MALLORCA
THAT YOU SHOULDN'T MISS
ISBN 978-3-95451-281-2

Peter Eickhoff
111 PLACES IN VIENNA
THAT YOU SHOULDN'T MISS
ISBN 978-3-95451-206-5

Frank McNally
111 PLACES IN DUBLIN
THAT YOU SHOULDN'T MISS
ISBN 978-3-95451-649-0

Gordon Streisand
111 PLACES IN MIAMI
AND THE KEYS
THAT YOU MUST NOT MISS
ISBN 978-3-95451-644-5

Marcus X. Schmid
111 PLACES IN ISTANBUL
THAT YOU MUST NOT MISS
ISBN 978-3-95451-423-6

Gerd Wolfgang Sievers
**111 PLACES IN VENICE
THAT YOU MUST NOT MISS**
ISBN 978-3-95451-460-1

Petra Sophia Zimmermann
**111 PLACES IN VERONA
AND LAKE GARDA THAT
YOU MUST NOT MISS**
ISBN 978-3-95451-611-7

Gillian Tait
**111 PLACES IN EDINBURGH
THAT YOU SHOULDN'T MISS**
ISBN 978-3-95451-883-8

Laurel Moglen, Julia Posey
**111 PLACES IN LOS ANGELES
THAT YOU SHOULDN'T MISS**
ISBN 978-3-95451-884-5

John Sykes
**111 PLACES IN LONDON
THAT YOU SHOULDN'T MISS**
ISBN 978-3-95451-346-8

Julian Treuherz, Peter de Figueiredo
**111 PLACES IN LIVERPOOL
THAT YOU SHOULDN'T MISS**
ISBN 978-3-95451-769-5

Annett Klingner
**111 PLACES IN ROME
THAT YOU MUST NOT MISS**
ISBN 978-3-95451-469-4

Kirstin von Glasow
**111 COFFEESHOPS IN
LONDON THAT YOU MUST
NOT MISS**
ISBN 978-3-95451-614-8

Giulia Castelli Gattinara, Mario Verin
**111 PLACES IN MILAN
THAT YOU MUST NOT MISS**
ISBN 978-3-95451-331-4

Rüdiger Liedtke, Laszlo Trankovits
**111 PLACES IN CAPE TOWN
THAT YOU MUST NOT MISS**
ISBN 978-3-95451-610-0

Jo-Anne Elikann
**111 PLACES IN NEW YORK
THAT YOU MUST NOT MISS**
ISBN 978-3-95451-052-8

Kathrin Bielfeldt, Raymond Wong,
Jürgen Bürger
**111 PLACES IN HONG KONG
THAT YOU SHOULDN'T MISS**
ISBN 978-3-95451-936-1

Nicola Perry, Daniel Reiter
33 Walks in London
Photographs by Daniel Reiter
ISBN 978-3-95451-886-9

Ralf Nestmeyer
**111 PLACES IN PROVENCE
THAT YOU MUST NOT MISS**
ISBN 978-3-95451-422-9

Beate C. Kirchner
**111 PLACES IN FLORENCE
AND NORTHERN TUSCANY
THAT YOU MUST NOT MISS**
ISBN 978-3-95451-613-1

Floriana Petersen, Steve Werney
**111 PLACES IN SAN FRANCISCO
THAT YOU MUST NOT MISS**
ISBN 978-3-95451-609-4

Ralf Nestmeyer
**111 PLACES ON THE
FRENCH RIVIERA
THAT YOU MUST NOT MISS**
ISBN 978-3-95451-612-4

Kirstin von Glasow
**111 SHOPS IN LONDON
THAT YOU SHOULDN'T MISS**
ISBN 978-3-95451-341-3

The author

Kai Oidtmann lives in Cologne, Germany, and writes for TV and radio. Despite his preference for a warm climate, Iceland delighted him from the very first moment. Spectacular natural beauty in the countryside, cultural diversity in towns, and people who stay calm under almost any circumstances – these things arouse his longing to visit Iceland.